THE
FIFTH PILLAR
A SPIRITUAL PILGRIMAGE

DAVID ZEIDAN

piquant

ARAB
WORLD
MINISTRIES

This revised edition copyright © 2000 Piquant
10 09 08 9 8 7 6 5

Published by Piquant
PO Box 83, Carlisle, CA3 9GR,
United Kingdom
Website: www.piquant.net
ISBN 978-0-9535757-4-9

First published in 1993 by Paternoster OM,
Carlisle, UK

Cover design by AWM Graphics

Designed by Gazelle Creative Productions Ltd
Printed and bound in Great Britain by CPI Bookmarque,
Croydon, CR0 4TD

Dedication

'Nabil' wishes to dedicate this book to his two sons in the hope that they will follow him along the path of truth. He dedicates it also to all his good friends who helped him, many of whom appear as characters in this story.

Contents

Note: The names of people and some places have been changed to protect vulnerable individuals.

Preface

This is a true story of spiritual pilgrimage.

From the day a person is born until the day they die, each person travels a unique path through life in this world. Some consciously seek for guidance and for an understanding of the true meaning of life; others seek it subconsciously. Some rebel at the thought that there may be a 'true meaning' to life; others submit to what God reveals to them on that journey.

At the start of his quest, Nabil had everything he could wish for - a good career, money, connections, respectability. Yet, something was missing. As he persevered in his search he discovered that the meaning of life is not found in a religious framework of commandments, rituals and traditions, but in a divine Person with whom he could have a personal relationship. He also discovered that there was a cost to pay for following that Person.

The Quarrel

'Do as you wish,' said Nabil Madani with little sign of concern as he leant back in the plush chair, 'my friends are my own personal affair and you have no right to interfere in my private life.'

Nabil's older brother, Anwar, and Nabil's boss, Ahmad, sat facing him across the coffee table in Nabil's comfortable apartment on the eighth floor of a high–rise building in a wealthy part of Dubai. The two men were getting more and more frustrated by trying to talk sense into this young man's head. Who did he think he was? How could he dare disobey their instructions and keep going his own independent way? This was an intolerable situation; it had to be stopped! They would not budge; if Nabil didn't submit to them, they would teach him a lesson he would never forget.

'Listen, Nabil,' said Anwar softly, stroking his dark beard, 'this is no joke. You have gone too far down this road; we cannot let you go on any further. These are our final conditions, and you better accept them: cut off all relationships with Henry and your other western friends and resume an orthodox Muslim way of life. This is all we are asking of you!'

'You have three weeks in which to make your decision,' added Ahmad. 'You know we are happy with your work; we only want what is best for you. You are a Muslim from a respectable family working for a Muslim publisher – you must be seen to live as a good Muslim. Surely we are not asking you for anything too much? For us there can be no compromise in this matter.'

'I certainly don't need you to tell me what to do,' retorted Nabil angrily. 'I won't attend prayers with you any longer, seeing you are trying to compel me to do it. You have no right to force religion down my throat.'

There followed a heated discussion. Ahmad and Anwar wouldn't give in, and Nabil responded to their aggressive tone with characteristic stubbornness. 'You'd better accept our terms,' they warned him, 'otherwise we'll reject you. See who will be your friends then, when you lose your job!'

The two men left the flat in an angry mood. Nabil felt the resentment exploding in him as they walked out. Just who did they think they were, trying to lay down the law for him in this way? He would show them that he was a free man, able to make his own independent choices. That snooty brother of his! He should not think that just because he was a year older than Nabil he could order him around. As far back as Nabil could remember it had always been like this – Anwar the goody–goody, always the one to be set up as a role model for Nabil. Nabil the regular guy, never good enough, never matching up to the shining example of his older brother. And how bigoted Anwar had become in his narrow, fundamentalist Islamic world view.

Nabil felt he had been a good Muslim, at least, as far as they were concerned, until recently. He had kept the five pillars of his religion faithfully, as well as most of the traditions. He was a religious man – but that didn't mean he had to ram it down other people's throats in the way these two were now doing to him.

This was the twentieth century, not the seventh!

As these thoughts milled in his mind, a shadow of doubt settled over Nabil. Was he maybe very naïve in his view of life? Was he just the spoilt younger son who could get whatever he wanted from his doting mother and sisters, and wheedle his way out of most confrontations with his stern father? Nabil had always assumed that religion was a personal affair, a private matter between him and God. But did this assumption fit the world of Islam? He had learned enough to realize that Islam is a religion which demands total submission to its teachings in all areas of life - there is no religious-secular divide in Islam or any private-versus-communal dichotomy. Islam is all-encompassing; it claims the rule of God's authority over every compartment of human living. 'Personal choice' is really a new-fangled western innovation, he realized, and opposes traditional Sunni Islam, which rules triumphantly and expects total obedience, a God-given duty that needs no apology! Nabil shuddered. He was slowly understanding the implications of his thoughts. What if the two men really meant their threats and were prepared to implement them? What a fool he had been! He should have been more careful, bent a little, negotiated – they would have accepted any attempt at a compromise as a sign of his repentance. Things could have returned to normal. Why had he been so stubborn? What would happen now?

The next day Nabil was full of apprehension as he approached his office. His brother had first introduced him to Ahmad three years earlier. At the time, Ahmad was looking for the right person to put in charge of the newly established Dubai branch of his successful

Islamic Publishing House, a prestigious publishing company with branches in all the Arabic and most of the Muslim countries. Nabil had gladly accepted the job, which offered excellent pay and career development opportunities.

Nabil proved to be a hard worker. He established sound management and accounting procedures, saw the sales figures grow and considered himself to be an upcoming businessman. Ahmad was very pleased with his employee. In actual fact, everyone was pleased with him – his father, his brother, his colleagues. And now, what was going wrong?

The next few weeks were tense ones for Nabil. There was no doubt that Ahmad's attitude to him had changed significantly. Ahmad now ignored Nabil when he saw him in the office, counteracted Nabil's decisions, disregarded his messages. It was quite clear that, as far as Ahmad was concerned, the special relationship he had had with Nabil was now dead.

The weeks passed by and Nabil went on as though nothing was wrong. If they thought he would resign, they were mistaken. Nabil felt safely protected by the contract he had signed which was not due re-negotiation for many more months. He had no intention of breaking contract. He was eager to make a success of his career. But he was feeling worried. What if Ahmad was to dismiss him? He needed to stay away from his home country Syria for only a few more months in order to complete the five years abroad that were required for exemption from otherwise compulsory military service. It would be impossible for him to survive in Dubai without a job. Without a job he would also not be able to get a visa for the United Arab Emirates, of which Dubai was a part. It would be extremely difficult to find another job in

Dubai if his former boss would refuse to give him a recommendation. He might even be deported!

Nabil finally decided to do something about the situation. He contacted the Syrian consul in Dubai and invited him to dinner. During the evening Nabil mentioned his father and told the consul of his predicament. There were only a few months left to complete his five-year period away from Syria. 'Come to my office tomorrow with all your papers,' the consul suggested.

When Nabil arrived at the consul's office the following day he was given an official document certifying that he had fulfilled his five years out of Syria. It was duly signed by the consul and carried his official stamp. What a relief! Nabil sent it off at once to his father in Damascus to be passed to the relevant military authorities. At least one problem was solved, thanks to his father's good name and influential connections.

A few weeks later Ahmad walked into the office one morning and said 'Thank you, Nabil, for your work with our company. I think it is time for you to leave.' He seemed quite unemotional about it.

'But you are obliged to give me six weeks notice,' Nabil objected. 'I have signed a contract that is valid for another four months. What about my outstanding salary? What about compensation? What about my holiday ticket and bonus? After all, I have worked here for over three years!'

'Oh, that will all be sorted out,' Ahmad replied smoothly. 'I've discussed it all with Anwar. Talk to him; he will arrange everything.'

Nabil left the office somewhat in a daze. So, they had finally fulfilled their threat. Should he contact

Anwar? He decided not to. Instead, he would wait till Anwar got in touch with him. In the meantime he returned to his flat and started packing his belongings. A couple of days later Anwar phoned to say he was coming to see Nabil. He brought his wife along. Anwar explained calmly that he himself had initiated the proceedings against Nabil because of his stubbornness and his refusal to obey their ultimatum. It served him right to have lost his job.

Nabil felt it would be futile to argue. Anwar had made up his mind; there was no going back. 'Can you see to it that I get my outstanding salary and all payments owed me?' he asked. 'Ahmad said you would arrange everything.'

'Oh,' replied Anwar with mock surprise, 'if you want to claim your rights you can take up the matter with the labour court. Ahmad refuses to pay you anything more.' Nabil realized that Anwar was being sarcastic. This was all part of the punishment they had devised for him. He would not have any chance of success in the labour court; the case would drag on for years and cost him a small fortune in legal fees. He had calculated that Ahmad still owed him some $15,000 – two months' salary, holiday bonuses, expenses – it was a large sum to lose, but it seemed nothing could be done about it now.

'Thank you for your help,' said Nabil bitterly. 'Would you be so kind as to store some of my belongings in your house?' Though Anwar agreed to that, they parted unreconciled. Anwar was angry at his younger brother's defiance. How could he be so independent and ignore the advice of his older brother and of his family? It was impudent and that was inexcusable. He had to be punished and left to stew in his own juice. Nabil had to be humiliated and broken – there was no other way of dealing with such a case. Anwar had no doubt that Nabil would finally break down, repent and apologize.

Anwar arranged for a truck to pick up Nabil's stuff, while Nabil rolled up his affairs in Dubai. His car was left with a good friend who promised to sell it and transfer the money to his account. When he had finished packing, he phoned for a taxi to the airport. There he boarded a plane scheduled for Warsaw. Warsaw, after all, was where Renata was waiting for him . . .

Nabil had come to a crucial decision. Until this moment he had thought he could live in two worlds. His brother's ultimatum showed him the folly of such thinking. It was suddenly a relief to be heading out of the turbulent life in the Middle East. As he thought of Renata he longed for the apparent security and stability of Communist Eastern Europe. However, as he relaxed into his seat, he could not stop the images that filled his mind, images from his family's history. He remembered details from his own life. So many faces passed by, so many things that had led up to this final quarrel and separation. Above all, he now needed time to think . . .

In the Mountain
of the Druze

Fairouz Madani sat distraught in a wicker chair in a shady corner of the balcony of her house in the small town of Suweida. It was summer; it was dry and dusty and the sun beat down mercilessly. Farouz was six months pregnant. She did not feel well, had not been feeling well since the start of this pregnancy. What were they doing here in this God-forsaken corner of southern Syria? If only they had stayed in Damascus, the beautiful capital city with all its amenities where all their family and friends lived! They had been so happy there during their first year of marriage, before Hasib was posted to Suweida, capital of the region known as Jebel ad-Druze, as an aide to the provincial governor.

Fairouz missed her family above all else. She had always been the centre of their close-knit family circle and, because of her lively and mature personality, her two brothers and three sisters often turned to her for advice, counselling and comfort. She enjoyed that position of quiet leadership; it came naturally to her. She really loved them all and, although most of them were now married, she enjoyed the rounds of visiting that are part of Arabic culture, binding the extended families firmly together. But since moving to Suweida they had returned to Damascus only once or twice a year for a brief visit during their annual holidays. Fairouz felt overcome by loneliness.

There was nothing Hasib could do about it. He held a very important position, and Fairouz knew that meant her husband was highly respected in the Ministry of Interior. Syria, in the process of reorganizing itself after independence, needed all its available qualified officials to work hard at maintaining the unity of the new state and building up an efficient bureaucracy, especially in the outlying provinces.

Fairouz was proud of Hasib. Like her, he came from the respectable Sunni upper class of Damascus. His family, originally from Turkey, had been living in Damascus for two centuries. Her own family had been living there as far back as anyone could trace it. It was a great honour to belong to these old families who had composed the ruling class of Syria ever since the Muslim conquest in the seventh century. These families had been the backbone of the glorious Umayad Caliphate period, when Damascus was established as the capital of the vast Islamic Empire that stretched from Spain in the west to India in the east.

In the 1940s Hasib had served as an officer in the French forces of mandatory Syria. After independence in 1946 he was posted to the Ministry of Interior in Damascus and put in charge of registration of all citizens of the new state, issuing them with identity cards. It was an important job, essential for organizing the new state's control over its diverse peoples and for creating an efficient tax base. Syria is a hodge-podge of diverse ethnic and religious groups - Sunnis, 'Alawis, Druze, Isma'ilis, Kurds, Turkomans, Christians - it would be no easy task to weld them all together into a functioning modern state! Hasib had done well and, as a result, was posted to this new position in Suweida.

Fairouz smiled to herself as she remembered how they had first met. It was funny. She had been standing at the second floor window of their family house in Damascus eating an apple as she looked out at the busy street scene below. For some reason the apple slipped from her hand and fell down almost on top of a man in uniform who was passing by at that very moment. He looked up angrily, opened his mouth to reprimand the careless culprit, but shut it in surprise when he looked into the lustrous dark eyes of a beautiful young girl with wavy black hair, staring down at him in shock at what she had done. Their eyes met, he smiled at her, waved his hand to imply it was nothing, and went on his way. She gazed dreamily after his tall, receding figure, remembering his good looks. He was impressive in his neat army uniform, obviously a high-ranking officer she had not met before.

Apparently the soldier did not forget the girl either, for some days later his mother visited her mother to find out more about their family. It wasn't long before both his parents visited her parents and officially asked for her hand in marriage to their son.

Hasib later told her that as soon as he got home he had gone straight to his mother and said, 'I saw a girl today; this is her address. Please visit her family – I want to marry her.' He was a man who acted decisively once he had made up his mind. It was a trait that Fairouz admired in Hasib. His parents had been looking at that time for a suitable girl for him to marry, so when they had checked her background and found out that Fairouz came from a respectable family, they were happy to proceed with all the arrangements to see their son happily married and settled down.

Marriage arrangements were made, according to

old custom, between the parents of the prospective bride and groom if they were happy that it would be a suitable match. Family connections were all-important - a person was expected to marry within their social class or above it, if at all possible! Respectability was essential; both sides spent much time checking the other family's background to make sure their own family honour would not be impaired by this alliance. Money was also of importance, for power and wealth were essential to maintain the important families of Damascus. It is said that blood is thicker than water, and once two families were linked by marriage they would be loyal to each other and committed to help all their members to advance socially, economically and politically by relying on their network of relatives and contacts in high places.

When Fairouz was finally asked for her consent, she gladly said yes - at least she had seen her prospective husband before she was asked, and liked what she had seen, which was more than some girls in her position could hope for.

They were married in 1955 and settled down to a carefree life in the capital city, enjoying a busy social schedule of parties, dances and visits to friends and family. That was, until Hasib was posted to his new position, faraway among the Druze people.

The Druze constituted only 3 per cent of Syria's population, a hardy warrior community living in the natural fortresses of the mountainous region near the Jordanian border. In the 1920s they had been the first people to rebel against French colonial power, igniting a fire of nationalism that soon swept up the Sunni Arabs of Damascus. The French retaliated by bombarding the city and there was fierce fighting before the rebellion was quelled. Yet now the Druze loyalty to the new 'independent' Syria was questionable. Some Druze suggested that their area be incorporated into the neighbouring kingdom of Jordan. As a heretical sect that emerged from Shi'a Islam a thousand years earlier, they had been badly treated by the Sunni rulers of Damascus through the ages. Their grudge against the ruling families could cause a renewed rebellion unless they were tactfully and firmly treated by the new regime.

Fairouz, one of the new generation of Syrian girls who had benefited from further education, was a trained teacher. Independence had brought with it high hopes of education for the masses and of Syria's accelerated advance, politically, economically and culturally, to become once again the leader of the Arab world. A high rate of illiteracy was inimical to this goal, and the new state was recruiting all its resources to combat this problem. In Suweida, Fairouz was doing her part to realize the Syrian ambition by teaching in the local elementary girls' school.

It was a fine feeling to have high hopes for your beloved country and be able to contribute to the achievement of them. However, Fairouz knew her family and friends did not think much of her job in Suweida. They considered jobs in the capital city only as having any prestige. The Damascenes had always looked down on the provincials. And now Fairouz was very weary and depressed. Their first son, Anwar, had been born just one year earlier and, though he was the pride of her life, she still hadn't regained her strength.

When she found out that she was pregnant again, she wept in despair. She had even tried to terminate the pregnancy by taking some pills the local doctor prescribed for her, but without success. The doctor then suggested she take a drive over the bumpy mountain roads in the area in the hope that it would trigger a miscarriage, and when that didn't work he sent her to the hot springs at al-Hama in the Yarmuk River valley. All to no avail. It was getting more and more difficult for her to wake up early each morning, trudge the distance to school and face the pupils for hours on end. She longed for a break, a rest, a change of scenery.

Fairouz did have a Druze maid, Sarah, who came in each day to do the cleaning and cooking and to take care of baby Anwar. As a simple country girl, Sarah was devoted to her and to the baby and did her work well. That was one thing about the Druze that Fairouz liked. If you won their loyalty they would support you through thick and thin. Sarah had even offered to adopt the unborn child to make things easier for Fairouz, but that of course was out of the question. A Madani child must be brought up in the strict Sunni Islamic faith of the family. It would be a great shame to give it over to be brought up in the heretical Druze faith, unthinkable!

The Druze were a fine people. But they were backward and clannish. The majority of them were simple peasants and, though they spoke Arabic and were Syrian citizens, Fairouz found their culture totally different from her own. They appreciated her work for them in education. They respected Hasib's government position. They visited and brought gifts of their farm produce, but she could get no closer to any of them. Their secret religion was a big barrier. Fairouz and Hasib were never invited to attend their prayers or religious activities, and the Druze would never speak to strangers about their faith.

As a result of the centuries of persecution, the Druze had become an introverted religious community that did not seek for converts. All they asked of the outside world was to be left alone with autonomy to run their own internal affairs and appoint their own designated religious leaders. In the past they had fought fiercely against all intruders to preserve their freedom and now they were feared and respected by the other communities of Syria and Lebanon.

In November 1957 Fairouz gave birth to her second son. There was no hospital at that time in Suweida, and the child was born at home, attended by a doctor and a midwife. Fortunately there were no complications. Though feeling very weak, Fairouz was glad to have another son and delighted to see Hasib's obvious pride when he first held the baby. It was a great honour to bear multiple sons; it meant the family name would continue. They called him Nabil.

A few months later Hasib received good news – he was to be relocated to Damascus. Fairouz felt her prayers had been answered; she looked forward to settling back into her beloved home city and once again leading a fulfilled life there.

Damascus,
Pearl of the East

In 1958 Hasib and Fairouz returned to Damascus with their two boys. Hasib had been given an important post as Director of the Population Registration Department in the Ministry of Interior, a post he was to hold for thirty years, until his retirement in 1988. It was well paid, he had an official car and chauffeur at his disposal and, most crucial for his career, he was in touch with the really important people in government circles. His future seemed secure.

They settled in a large flat in the modern quarter of Mazra'a. It was near the main government offices and the diplomatic quarters. In the distance they could see the peaks of the Anti-Lebanon and the 2800 m high snow-capped summit of Mt. Hermon. The Barada River (the Abana, mentioned in the Bible) flows down from those mountains and through Damascus to provide a green oasis in the desert, all year round. The city was surrounded by the gardens and orchards of the famous al-Ghutah oasis, criss-crossed by the many channels that irrigated it. No wonder that to the ancient Beduin, coming out of the barren desert, Damascus and its surroundings seemed like a glimpse of Paradise; according to tradition it is the site of the original Garden of Eden! There is a Hadith attributed to the Prophet Muhammad that says 'blessed is he who owns but the area of a tent stake in Damascus'.

There were wide tree-lined streets in the quarter where the Madani family settled and they were within easy walking distance of the old city with its colourful market and famous old buildings. Damascus is a historic city, considered to be the oldest inhabited city on earth. Egyptians, Hittites, Arameans, Assyrians, Babylonians, Persians, Greeks, Romans, Byzantines, Arabs, Mameluks, Turks, French – all had ruled there for a while, and each had left their mark on the place. But it is the Islamic religion and the Arabic language that finally survived and established Damascus as the capital of an independent Arabic Syrian state.

There were old churches from the Roman and Byzantine periods, and the glorious Great Umayad Mosque, the earliest surviving stone mosque in the world, built by the Caliph a-Walid I between 705 and 715. Everywhere there were reminders of ancient times, buildings constructed by famous men, tombs of great rulers and of saints. It was no wonder the Damascenes regarded themselves proudly as the elite, not only of Syria, but of the whole Arab world. They looked down scornfully on the 'uncivilized' citizens of the other Syrian towns such as Aleppo, Homs and Hama as well as on the simple village folk and the nomadic desert Beduin.

Now that Hasib and Fairouz were living close to both their families they had a busy schedule of mutual visiting and entertaining. Hasib, as eldest brother, was recognized as head of the extended family. His brothers and sisters deferred all projects, problems and decisions to him, and his word was final. They showed him much respect, kissed his hand when greeting him and asked for his blessing when leaving. This is the accepted way in Muslim Syrian society, which is strongly patriarchal, the eldest male having ultimate authority in the family and clan. Fairouz had always been the centre of her own family before she married.

Now her brothers and sisters again came to her for counsel and support.

Though they were faithful Sunnis of the Shafi'i school, Hasib and Fairouz weren't very religious. They enjoyed parties, dancing and going out, seeing themselves as modern Muslims who could combine the best of the West with the best in Islam. However, on their return to Damascus they soon fell under the influence of Fairouz's brother, Muhammad, who visited them a lot. Muhammad was a lawyer by profession who had gone on to study Islam under the famous 'Abd al-Krim Rifa'i in the Shari'a University of Damascus, and later at the famous al-Azhar Islamic University in Cairo. He had returned to Damascus as an extremely devout and fanatical Muslim, full of reforming zeal for bringing Islam back to its pristine glory and converting all Muslims to their pure and strict old-fashioned faith.

Muhammad had a charismatic personality. His zeal was very contagious. Under his influence Hasib started visiting the mosque regularly, saying his prayers and keeping all the rituals. Fairouz gave up her teaching in order to devote herself to her home and children, as required by traditional Islamic rules. Both eventually came to accept Muhammad's fundamentalist views as the truth. Only on one issue did Fairouz resist her persuasive brother - she would not wear the traditional veil. He himself was so strict that he would not let any male member of his own family see his wife - only the women and children had access to her.

As a teacher, Fairouz could help train her children from a young age. Hasib and she had great hopes and plans for them and wanted them to succeed in life. At three years of age Anwar was sent to a private Muslim nursery school and one year later Nabil went too. Here they got a good grounding in reading and writing. They had such a good head start that when they moved to a regular school at the age of five, they were put straight into the second grade.

Fairouz subsequently in Damascus gave birth to three girls, Jamileh, Amal and Iman. They were a close-knit family; Fairouz flourished in the security of her beloved Damascus and coped well with the responsibilities of her growing family. It seemed that she had developed a mild heart condition whilst in Suweida, but she managed her duties and, above all, was once again at the centre of her family and acquaintances. This was the world she knew and loved and was most comfortable in.

Religion gave the family stability and a sense of belonging to the great Islamic nation, the umma, whilst Hasib's job made them part of the upper class of Syrian society. They were looked up to and respected by their neighbours. They had 'arrived'.

Hasib was a stern father. He believed in old-fashioned virtues coupled with military-like discipline. Obedience was expected and enforced. When he decided on something, no cajoling would make him change his mind! Children could not joke with their father or treat him as a friend; children had to treat both parents with respect and decorum. They kissed their father's hand when greeting him and turned their eyes down when speaking to him. They were not allowed to sit with their parents' visitors unless specifically asked to join them. They had to ask for their parents' blessing every time they met them. Islam teaches that respect for parents and obedience to them is equivalent to respect for and obedience to

God himself. As it is written, 'You will not even say uffa to them,' meaning you will not answer them back in any way.

Hasib organized the children's life in a strict way. Every minute had to be accounted for. Each child received a weekly allowance, and it was no use begging for more if you had spent it all during the first days of the week; not a cent was forthcoming until the next pay-day.

Family ties were very strong in the Madani household. Their social life now revolved mainly around extended families on both sides, with much cross-visiting and entertaining. Their former worldly pleasures were shunned and forbidden to the children growing up. Instead, the family and the mosque were now seen as their natural environment, centres and shelters for the devout.

Fairouz spent much time coaching the children through their homework; Hasib would check their work and supervise how they spent their time. The children were given all they needed. Each boy had his own corner with an own desk, chair and shelves where they could study and do homework without being disturbed. This emphasis on education bore fruit and both boys did very well at school. Anwar distinguished himself as a brilliant scholar; Nabil was always top of his class, often chosen to be the teacher's aide and given tasks such as arranging the chairs, cleaning the blackboard and checking for absent students, a position considered a special privilege.

Having decided to take religion seriously, Hasib, true to nature, threw his whole being into it. He would visit the mosque to perform his prayers (salat), not just those commanded by Muhammad for the dawn and sunset ceremonies, but five times a day as prescribed by tradition. He saw to it that all members of the family also kept strictly to the prescribed prayer times. If at home, for some reason unable to go to the mosque, he would gather them all, even at 4 o'clock in the morning, for the dawn prayer. He would stand in front, the two boys behind him, and Fairouz and the girls in the last row, all facing Mecca and devoutly repeating the familiar formulas while prostrating themselves before God.

The Ramadan fast was strictly kept in the Madani household. Fairouz would get up early in the morning, before the sun had risen, to prepare the early breakfast S'hur. Everyone got up before dawn to eat together. Then, as soon as the muezzin called to announce the rising of the sun, everyone, including the children, would fast from food and drink until after sunset when they broke their fast together as a family. They would pray together, standing in rows behind Hasib, before going to the mosque where a special prayer had to be repeated twenty times.

According to Islamic law children are supposed to start fasting from the age of seven. Between seven and nine they can break the fast earlier than adults, but from nine years onwards they must fast the whole day or be beaten! Hasib awarded money to those who completed the fast, though the children would often cheat, have a quick bite and sip of water in the bathroom, but swear they never touched a morsel all day just to get the prize. It was especially hard when Ramadan fell in the summer time, with such intense heat. Smokers seemed worse affected and one of their uncles, a heavy smoker, would often lose his temper and start swearing and cursing about the folly of fasting. People would respond by saying 'How dare you use such language in Ramadan? It is better if you eat and shut up!'

At the end of Ramadan came the three-day feast of 'Id al-Fitr. The children were off school for this holiday. In preparation for the feast they were entitled to accompany their parents to the market to choose a new set of clothes and shoes for themselves. Adults who visited gave them gifts of money, and the children competed to see who would collect the most. Invariably, Anwar was the winner, as gifts would be given according to age, followed by Nabil and, lastly, the girls. Nabil was upset because he could never catch up with his older brother. He needed the money just as much as Anwar. He experienced this with a deep sense of unfairness! The money usually lasted for quite a while and was used mainly to purchase chocolates and sweets from the school tuckshop.

Fairouz would be busy in the kitchen, many days before the feast, to prepare the large quantities of food and the delicious Ma'moul cakes - she would bake three to four hundred of them! Every visitor had to eat something before they left. At the time of this feast it was also customary to visit family, and Hasib, Fairouz and the children would dutifully visit grandparents, uncles and aunts. On return to school, there was great excitement as the children exchanged stories and compared what they had received during the feast. Another important aspect of this feast was that of giving alms to the poor, called zakat al-Fitr. Hasib had to pay a certain amount for each member of his family and distribute the money to needy families. He and Fairouz would sit together to draw up a list of those who had the greatest need, so that they could pass the money to them before the first day of feasting.

'Id al-Adha, the four-day feast to celebrate the end of that year's pilgrimage to Mecca, was another important festival to which the children looked forward. They were off school for this feast too, and once again adults had to provide new clothes and money gifts - it was like having two Christmases each year! Hasib would ask an uncle to buy a sheep for the family. Then the butcher would come around to slaughter the sacrificial sheep ritually for everyone in the neighbourhood. Hasib would read a few verses from the Qur'an, the slaughterer would say 'Bism'illah' ('in the Name of God') and cut the throat of the sheep, letting all the blood flow out into the street. The women and children would watch from the balconies. Later they would go down to wash the street clean. The butcher would then skin the sheep and cut it up for the family – Fairouz would keep 10 per cent of the best cuts to cook for themselves; the rest had to be wrapped up in neat packages to give to several needy families in the area. Anwar and Nabil had the job of distributing the packages.

It is important for a Muslim to perform all the religious rituals and to do good deeds, such as giving to the poor. It is believed that this will greatly increase a person's chances to get into Paradise when the terrible Day of Judgement arrives; one's good deeds will be balanced against one's bad ones. It is believed that every deed is recorded and remembered. It can never do harm to increase one's store of good deeds and to gain as much merit as possible while one still has the chance.

Muhammad's Birthday, Mawlad al-Nabawwi, was also celebrated in a big way. Every mosque would set out chairs in the street and string up special lights and green banners with verses glorifying the prophet. The radio and TV stations would broadcast the service from the great mosque in Damascus, attended by the President himself. In the afternoon everyone would go to their local mosque for a special service of chanting and prayers. A small bag of sweets, wrapped in cellophane, would be distributed to all who attended the mosque.

The religious feasts were celebrated at home and in the mosque. At school they celebrated the national feasts - especially Independence Day, on 17 July, and Revolution Day, on 8 March. The classrooms would be decorated, there would be speeches and recitals of poems glorifying the state and its leaders. For Nabil the enjoyable part was that there were no classes, no lessons and no homework!

Growing up with Islam

Although Hasib attended some religious instruction classes at the mosque, he did not feel called to immerse himself in the intricacies of Islamic theology to the same extent as Muhammad was doing. Muhammad eventually got into trouble with the authorities because of his activities with the Muslim Brotherhood. During the rule of Nur al-Din Attassi, the Government ordered a crackdown on the Brotherhood, and soon they were looking for Muhammad. Hasib came to his aid by hiding him in his house for a few days and then helping him get out of the country to flee to Saudi Arabia. There Muhammad eventually got a job in the Saudi Ministry of Education and settled in Medina.

After school hours the boys attended an Islamics course at the Zayd Mosque in the old part of the city. This mosque served as an Islamic Centre; it offered courses for various age groups as well as conference facilities. Throughout the summer holidays the boys had to attend these classes - they certainly did not always feel like it, but never dared disobey their father. At best they would sometimes escape for an hour or two with other boys to play in the nearby streets. The teacher would report them to their fathers, and they would get a scolding or a tug of the ear for their frivolity.

Day after day Anwar and Nabil had to trudge to the mosque where, from 4pm till 8pm, they had to memorize passages from the Qur'an, study the Hadith, the Sunnah and Fiqh. Anwar seemed to enjoy these studies much more than Nabil and gained much admiration for his religious zeal and knowledge. Nabil found it all rather boring but did what was required of him. He was especially zealous to memorize the Qur'an - Hasib paid 35 Syrian cents for every page memorized! Eventually Nabil knew at least three-quarters of the Qur'an by heart.

Hasib kept a close eye on the Damascan schools to make sure his boys were attending only the very best. This meant they had to change schools several times, and Hasib used his government position and connections to get the necessary authorization for these changes, changes that were not available to ordinary citizens.

Nabil enjoyed sports. He played basketball, football and volleyball. He also liked Arabic and maths, but he could never keep up with his older brother who was considered to be a model student. Anwar was diligent and pious and, though he loved him, Nabil found him a bit of a prig. He couldn't share his personal thoughts with Anwar and had to find friends at school who would understand him and share his boyish interests. Hasib also registered the boys at the local library and they had to brief him regularly about what they were reading.

The Madani boys weren't allowed to play at school or on the streets after school hours like other children. They weren't allowed to walk around the streets with their friends or even visit them in their homes without explicit permission. Hasib wanted to know who these friends were, and made sure they kept only the very best company - boys from respectable, well-off Sunni families. They could go out only when accompanied by their parents.

The boys were forbidden to visit Christians or to invite them home. Christians were considered impure, eaters of pork and drinkers of alcohol, worshippers of three Gods, guilty of the worst possible sin - that of Shirk, joining a man to God, thus giving the Almighty a partner. Christians were also considered to be the proprietors of the shady night spots of Damascus – the bars, nightclubs and discotheques that no reputable Muslim would ever frequent.

Hasib's chauffeur, supplied by the Ministry, was a Christian named Joseph. They had a working relationship, but no social contact. Joseph apparently lived up to the stereotype of the immoral Christian, interested only in where he could buy the cheapest drinks or which cabaret to visit that night. His wife even went out alone with one of his friends, an act that would be unthinkable for a devout Muslim woman.

In junior high school Nabil became very friendly with a Christian boy called Raymond. One day he invited Raymond to visit the Madani home and then, belatedly, asked Fairouz's permission. 'What is his name?' she asked.

'Raymond,' replied Nabil.

'He is a Christian,' she concluded (the name gave it away), 'I won't allow him to enter this house.'

'Why?' persisted Nabil stubbornly, to which the only answer was a slap across the face for daring to question her parental authority. The next few days Nabil had to invent various excuses as to why it was inconvenient for Raymond to visit their home, until the matter was forgotten.

So the boys grew up in a very protected environment, circumscribed by religion and family ties. Nabil resented this extreme strictness. He often felt ashamed in front of peers who were allowed more freedom, but there was nothing he could do about it. He also battled with feelings of jealousy towards Anwar, the favourite, the model son who, as eldest, always got the best deal, in furniture, clothes, bicycles, whatever; while Anwar got things brand-new, Nabil had to be content with his brother's handed down belongings. It really wasn't fair to be Number Two!

Hasib could have advanced his career very fast had he not become a fundamentalist Muslim. The Ba'ath party was in the ascendancy, and most government officials joined the party in order to further their careers. Hasib was invited to join, but refused. He liked their development policies and their militant anti-Israel stance, but he couldn't accept their anti-religious ideology. For that reason he had to watch on the sidelines as some of his friends advanced to ministerial positions while he stayed in the same post for many years. It was frustrating, but he was a man of principle and wouldn't give in. As a Sunni he was also galled by the ascendancy of the 'Alawis into the key positions of influence and especially with the installation of Hafiz Assad as President.

It was the curse of Syria, he thought, to have so many small splinter-communities living within its borders. The Sunnis composed over 60 per cent of the population and had always been the ruling class, but Syria was a mixture of many religious and ethnic minority groups, each leading its own separate communal life. A person's life was determined by the community they were born into. There was no scope for intermarriage or change of identity. You were expected to be loyal, first and foremost, to your own community. Pan-Syrian nationalism was a modern innovation, which could be tolerated as long as it did not run counter to the deep-set traditional loyalties.

The 'Alawis, the Druze and the Isma'ilis had all emerged from the ancient Shi'a groups of Islam who revered 'Ali and his descendants as semi-divine figures, a belief abhorrent to all believing Sunnis. The 'Alawis were the largest minority group, comprising 13 per cent of the total population. They lived mainly in the northwest region of Syria, called Jebel al-Ansariya, and had been cruelly persecuted as heretics by the Sunnis for many centuries. Now there was an opportunity for revenge.

South of the 'Alawis lived the Isma'ilis, a much smaller community whose ancestors had at one time almost gained control of the whole Muslim world. During the Crusader period they had been notorious as the sect of the Assassins led by the 'Old Man of the Mountain', and all Middle Eastern rulers, Muslims and Christians alike, had lived in fear of their daggers.

The Kurds, comprising around 10 per cent of the Syrian population, lived mainly in the northeast. Though they were Sunni Muslims, they were not Arabs, but spoke their own Kurdish language and had their own ancient tribal culture. They were kept under constant, tight supervision by the security forces because of their penchant for autonomy.

There were also Turkomans, Turkish-speaking tribal groups who had swept into Anatolia from Central Asia and conquered the Byzantine Christians.

The Christian communities in Syria composed around 10 per cent of the population, most of them descended from the ancient inhabitants of Syria, who had dwelt there as long as living memory. They had been Christianized during the Roman period and split into rival churches during the Byzantine era. Persecuted by the official Greek Orthodox state church, the Aramaic(Syriac)-speaking Jacobite and Nestorian churches had welcomed the Muslim conquerors as liberators. They retained their old rituals and used Aramaic as their liturgical language. Whoever were in charge of the central government needed a very delicate balancing act to rule this mixture of ethnic and religious groups.

For Nabil, high school was an exciting time. He was now allowed a little more independence from his parents and could spend more time with his school friends, studying with them after school hours, preparing for exams or working on projects. For the first time he came into contact with the outside world and with world views, ways of thinking, that differed from his own.

Due to Hasib's preoccupation with getting only the very best for his children, Nabil attended three different high schools in Damascus. The last one was the famous Jawdat al-Hashemi school, housed in the imposing building of the former parliament during the French mandate and named after a Syrian national hero. This was a school for the children of the best families in Damascus - high government officials, diplomats, army officers and the most wealthy businessmen. Pupils were dropped off in the morning by shining Mercedes limousines or sporty Porsches, luxurious status symbols. Nabil was ashamed of his father's drab ministerial car and would ask Joseph to drop him off some distance from the school so his friends couldn't see their car.

Sometimes Nabil would join other boys from his class to play truant and go into the town centre to hang around or visit a cinema. When discovered, they would be brought before the headmaster who demanded that their fathers came to see him. It was a standing joke that most of these fathers held such powerful positions that the teachers and the headmaster were afraid of doing anything to their precious offspring!

But life continued to be structured by Islam. Nabil had to keep all the rituals, which his parents enforced as his duty to God. Every evening Hasib would ask, 'Did you say your prayers at the appointed times?' When he had missed them, Nabil was too afraid to own up. Sometimes, if Hasib was suspicious, Nabil would have to prove his statement and he would recruit one of his sisters as a false witness to the fact that he had faithfully performed his religious duties. Amal was his favourite sister and she would often stand in for him when he faced trouble.

Lying soon became an easy way out of these difficult situations and Nabil had to invent excuses by the dozen to slither through the cross-examinations. More and more he came to view religion as a burdensome ritual that had to be kept out of fear for the consequences. Honesty didn't pay, because there was no forgiveness for any misconduct; punishment was always severe. Deception was the best way to escape trouble. Deception now marred what used to be a happy family life.

There were a few Christian pupils in Nabil's class, and Nabil became very friendly with Edmund, whose father held a high position in Government, so that Hasib could not forbid Nabil's visiting him. He would sometimes go to Edmund's home after school to study with him. Edmund's family would invite him to stay and have a meal with them and he sometimes accepted. He noticed that these Christians, whom he had been taught to despise, had an easier relationship with their parents and were much more relaxed about their religion. They were not dominated by fear, but enjoyed honesty and trust. They were free to tell their parents the truth about where they had been and what they had done. They attended church not because they were compelled to do so but because they wanted to. Nabil wondered about this. What made the difference?

Anwar's experience of high school was quite different. He joined the Muslim Union and regularly attended prayer and Qur'anic instruction classes. Hasib, who noticed the difference between his two sons, would often scold Nabil and say, 'You have the wrong set of friends and they have a bad influence on you. Keep away from them. Try to be like your brother – he has the right kind of friends and I can trust him to perform his religious duties. I don't have to ask him where he's been or what he's done – I know he's okay.' This made Nabil feel inferior and rejected. Why was Anwar so much better than him? Why was he always the good boy and Nabil, the black sheep of the family? It just wasn't fair!

In spite of these problems, Nabil graduated with good grades, but not good enough for Hasib! Anwar had graduated top of his class and started studying Civil Engineering at Damascus University. Hasib had hoped Nabil would do the same – engineering was at that time considered the most prestigious study course in Syrian universities. Only top grades were good enough to be accepted by the engineering faculties. The Government needed these graduates;

they received the highest salaries and were well respected. Nabil's grades were simply not good enough to be admitted to an engineering faculty. According to tradition, a family council was called together to discuss the matter.

Nabil suggested that he would go abroad and study in the United States or Britain, as some of his friends were planning to do, but Hasib and Fairouz were set against it. The decadent West would have a bad influence on him, and he would be out of their control. It was finally decided that Nabil should register at Damascus University for Accountancy studies. As compulsory military service was deferred for students until the end of their course, Anwar and Nabil were free to enjoy their student years.

Anwar performed very well at University. He got the highest grades and won several medals. He was also actively involved with Muslim student groups and, unbeknown to his father, became a member of the extremist Muslim Brotherhood. Nabil, on the other hand, had more 'ordinary' friends. They enjoyed going out to parties, dances, discos and picnics. Studies were not all-important; life was to be enjoyed; and what better time to enjoy life than during one's student days?

Hasib and Fairouz were worried about their younger son. He wasn't taking his religion seriously enough; something had to be done about it. They warned Nabil of the dangers of hellfire and exhorted him to pray and study the Qur'an regularly. They reminded him that there was no forgiveness for sins of omission or commission – the only possibility was to compensate by doing enough good deeds to tip the balance in one's favour. Two angels were busy registering all his bad deeds and all his good ones, he was reminded, and only on the final Day of Judgement would the result be known. He'd better do his best, or it could be too late! They referred to Anwar as an example in having chosen the right set of friends; they considered him wise. They reminded Nabil of his piety as a child and of the fact that he had learnt almost the whole Qur'an by heart. Why had he changed? Couldn't he simply follow their example and be content?

Finally, towards the end of his first year at university, they had another family council to discuss what to do with Nabil. Parents, elder brother and stern uncle, on a visit from Saudi Arabia, all gathered together to find a way out. Muhammad, his fanatically religious uncle, finally had an inspiration: send the boy on the pilgrimage (Haj) to Mecca! Surely this highest of all religious duties and experiences will purify his soul from all attachment to worldly pleasures. God will work there in his heart and change him to become like his brother and uncle. According to Muslim belief a person who had been on the Haj is a new-born person – all their sins have been washed away. The family's goal was to see Nabil stop wearing jeans, start growing a beard and be a perfect Muslim, keeping all the traditions and commandments. They would give anything to see this happen.

Nabil resisted the idea with all his might. He was only nineteen years old and the Haj was for old men! It was supposed to atone for the sins of a lifetime – so why not wait until he was fifty years old and had accumulated a respectable burden of sins that would make the Haj worthwhile and expiate all his sins at the same time! His friends would laugh at him if he went now. Anyway, he was a good enough Muslim. He believed in the One God and in his Prophet. He prayed pretty regularly and gave alms to the poor. He fasted during Ramadan – what more did they want of him?

But the family ignored Nabil and continued with their plans. The arrangements were made and the tickets were bought, leaving him no option. His friends at University joked and laughed about it. What a young Haji! It was really embarrassing, but there was no way out. So, one bright day in the autumn of 1976, Nabil was driven to the assembly point for the pilgrimage, given his money and documents and accompanied to the bus that would take him all the way to the holy city of Mecca.

The Haj

Nabil left Damascus in one of six buses, a convoy especially organized for Syrians going on the pilgrimage to Mecca. They travelled overland, taking the ancient route via Amman and Ma'an in Jordan, on to Tabouk in Saudi Arabia and then on to Mecca via Medina.

The convoy was well-organized – there were water tanks in every bus, a leader was appointed to take care of any problems, a separate truck transported all the luggage and an ambulance and medical team, consisting of a doctor and nurse, accompanied the convoy.

Traditionally it has been the responsibility of the ruler of Damascus to organize the caravans from his city, which was the assembly point for Muslims making the pilgrimage from all over Syria, Iraq, Iran and even farther East. For more than 1300 years camel caravans of pilgrims have been travelling from Syria to Mecca for the annual Haj. Millions of pilgrims from almost every country in the world converge yearly on the Holy City to express their membership of the worldwide umma (nation) of Islam and to complete this 'Pillar' of their faith.

The convoy travelled across the vast, featureless desert for four days. The pilgrims were very excited when they finally arrived in Mecca 'the blessed', the 'Mother of Cities', the centre of the Muslim world. It was a moving experience, a privilege for which some worshippers had saved up a lifetime.

Nabil's group was allocated rented flats in a building situated near the Sacred Mosque. There they could refresh themselves and change into the special white garments (ihram) worn by all pilgrims. Then they followed their guide into the great Mosque to comply with their first duty – to circle the Ka'aba seven times. The Ka'aba is in the centre of the Mosque. It is the most sacred shrine of Islam and represents the heart of Muslim piety.

Nabil didn't change into the compulsory white robe; he went dressed in jeans and a T-shirt. Hasib had commanded him to buy the appropriate garment immediately on arrival in Mecca, but he ignored that advice. He assumed he could do it later, a childish act of rebelliousness, of trying to be different, of saying, 'Does it really matter?' His companions were not pleased with him; they were shocked! On his first sight of the Ka'aba, Nabil stopped to utter a purely personal and selfish prayer, remembering how his mother had emphasized that a wish uttered at a person's first sight of the Shrine was sure to be granted by God. He had not dared look out of the bus window when they approached the town centre for fear of accidentally noticing the Mosque and so losing the opportunity to make this special wish!

When Nabil tried to enter the great Mosque, which accommodates 300,000 people, one of the special guards at the gate spotted him and he received a blow on the head from the guard's truncheon. He was ordered out and told to return only if appropriately dressed in the white ihram. Instead of obeying, however, he simply slipped in through another gate where the guards didn't notice him as the crowd surged past. By this time Nabil had lost his group. It was no use looking for them amongst the masses of people thronging around the Ka'aba in the open central plaza. The only thing to do was to perform the ceremonies on his own and then meet up with them later at the appointed meeting place outside the Mosque. Inside the holiest shrine of Islam, Nabil felt elated. This was God's House and, according to the teaching of Islam, the place Abraham had been commanded to build for God. Nabil felt that he was indeed in the very presence of this holy and all-powerful God.

Seven times he circled the shrine, taken up in the slow-moving current of worshippers flowing in an anti-clockwise direction around the holy Ka'aba as they recited Qur'anic verses and called out the prayer of submission to God specially commanded for this occasion, 'Labbayka, Allahumma, Labbayka. Labbayka, la sharika lak. Labbayka, inna al-hamda wal-ni'imata lak, wal-mulk' ('At your service, my God, at your service. You have no partner, yours the praise and the grace and the kingdom').

Nabil was overwhelmed with emotion. All the pilgrims wanted to get close enough to the shrine so that they could touch and kiss it, for these actions earn a person special merit and forgiveness. It is believed that the bodies of those who have kissed the Black Stone will never touch hellfire, not even if angels should try to throw them in! It was difficult and dangerous to force one's way into the inner circle nearest the shrine. Every year some people are trampled to death by the crushing crowds, propelled by the pressure from those behind them. The nearer one gets to the centre, the worse the shoving and pushing become.

Some African pilgrims had figured out a failproof technique for getting close enough to touch the shrine. They formed a circle, with the strongest men on the outside, the women and children inside. Those on the outside then linked hands and advanced, powerfully swinging their arms up and down to the beat of their prayers. Woe to anyone who tried to push through this moving fence of arms - if they should fall down there was little chance of their ever getting up again!

Other pilgrims had brought their own coffins with them. They paid to have these washed in the water of the holy Zemzem well and, after that, to have them touch the wall of the Ka'aba for a few moments. On return home they would instruct their families to make sure that when they die they are buried in these coffins, which would give them eternal protection from hellfire.

The guide had given Nabil's group good advice before entering the shrine, 'Don't take any cash or valuables in with you; there are always pick-pockets working in the crowd. If you see someone falling down, don't bend or kneel to help them - it may be the last thing you do! Just keep moving on, it's the guards' duty to try and save them.'

Nabil managed to reach the wall of the Ka'aba and touch its heavily embroidered silk covering (the Kiswa), of which a new one is brought each year by the pilgrims from Egypt. But Nabil did not manage to get near the Black Stone, believed to have been placed there by Adam. He completed the seven rounds and felt quite pleased with himself. Then he went to a clearly indicated nearby spot, where Abraham is reported to have prayed. Nabil prayed there. These prayers also earn the pilgrim merit for the Day of Judgement. Then Nabil stopped by the holy Zemzem well, where he drank the hallowed water and said another prayer. Next he went to Safa' and Marwa, the spots believed to mark the location of two hills between which Hagar supposedly ran up and down seven times in search of water after Abraham had left her in the desert with Ishmael. The distance between the two hills is half-a-mile, and Nabil walked or ran the distance seven times, as prescribed. All these holy places are enclosed within the space of the great Mosque, a vast area covered by marble and stone, air-conditioned and, even by modern standards, impressive. Having completed the duties of the first day, Nabil returned to his room.

The group stayed in Mecca for two more days. It was very hot. Nabil found the water unpalatable and preferred Pepsi or Coca Cola. Some families invited him to share their meals in a spirit of true Arab hospitality. Five times a day they would all join the crowds in the Mosque for the prayer ceremonies.

On the fourth day after arrival they were taken by bus to Mina, some miles out of Mecca, where all the pilgrims camped for two days to prepare for the main ceremony of the Haj. The two days are spent reciting the Qur'an, praying and listening to preachers. The vast camp of tents was set up in sections according to country and group. The flag of each state flew from a tall pole at the centre of each section; this made it easy to find one's way around. Nabil's group was taken to their special corner of the Syrian camp, where they met other Syrian pilgrims. The leader of the mosque in the area of Damascus where Nabil lived, was especially pleased to see him and took him under his wing (later, in 1984, this man had to flee from Syria to Saudi Arabia because of his involvement with the Muslim Brotherhood).

From this camp, on the ninth day of the Muslim pilgrimage month Dhu al-Hijjah, after shaving off some of his hair and cutting his fingernails, and now dressed in a clean white garment that left his right shoulder bare, Nabil walked the distance of three miles to the place where, according to tradition, Abraham and Muhammad defeated the devil. Every worshipper had to throw stones at a pillar representing Shaitan (Satan) while making sure they stayed out of the way of the stones thrown with great force by other pilgrims. Next the crowd of worshippers moved to Mt. 'Arafat, the Mount of Mercy.

This ninth day is the most important day of the pilgrimage. The duties of this day are laid down in the Qur'an as obligatory - everything else is the tradition of the Sunna. Some people fly to Mecca to attend this one day only in order to fulfil their pilgrimage duties, if they are unable to spare the time for the full pilgrimage period. Every person who has completed the rites of this day is entitled to the title 'Haj' and is highly respected on their return home.

From Mt. 'Arafat they returned to the camp, now filled with hundreds of thousands of people from every corner of the Muslim world, all concentrated in this one place. The remainder of this very holy day was spent in further reciting of prayers and listening to preachers. However, Nabil was quite shocked when he realized at one point that the preacher was talking about politics rather than about religion and was criticizing the Syrian Government for not being more extreme in their Muslim character. The preacher became more and more excited, which affected the listeners so that some of them became quite hysterical. Women screamed and wept; one man fainted and had to be taken away for medical treatment. This bothered Nabil. He thought it portrayed very bad taste and made an unfitting end to such a holy day.

On that particular holy day, an unusual thing happened. It had been a hot and sunny afternoon with not a cloud in the sky. Suddenly a cloud appeared, as from nowhere, and soon it poured with rain, a most unexpected phenomenon for the Mecca area at that time of the year. People quickly interpreted this as a sign from God to show his mercy and his approval of their Haj. Even on his return to Damascus, Nabil found people still talking about this special sign at the Haj and passing on rumours about it.

The worshippers returned to Mecca after that. There they again visited the Mosque to circle the Ka'aba seven times and to run the distance from Safa' to Marwa another seven times. But, while those around him were weeping with emotion at God's special grace and presence, Nabil no longer felt any special joy or peace or any emotion. He performed the duties, but without his heart being in it, and his experience certainly did not match the frenzy of the crowds.

Then the Haj was over; Nabil had performed it all. He was now officially a Haji. He would be called Haj Nabil Madani. What a strange feeling!

The next day the pilgrims returned to Mina for the four day 'Id al-Adha (Feast of Sacrifice) ceremonies that mark the end of the Haj period. Nabil bought a sheep at the market and hired someone to slaughter it for him ritually, as required for the sacrifice. He could only eat a small portion of the meat, as the remainder was supposed to be given to the poor, though most people around him had their sheep roasted and were happily eating away. Nabil mused on the enormous waste of good meat that couldn't be kept from spoiling in the hot climate. So much was simply thrown away.

Nabil then joined the part of his group who where going to Medina, the second holiest city of Islam, while the others headed straight back to Damascus. It was a 425-kilometre journey to Medina. On arrival they were put up in rented flats in the city centre, near the Mosque of the Prophet (Masjad ash-Sharif), which holds Muhammad's tomb. Nabil was soon met by his Uncle Muhammad, who lived in Medina and had come to pick him up. His uncle took him to see Muhammad's tomb in the centre of the green-domed Mosque that could easily hold a quarter of a million people.

There is a special ritual, the Ziyyarah, prescribed for a first visit to this mosque. It starts at the Gate of Peace and involves reciting special prayers at specified points. Nabil entered into the spirit of prayer. Having heard so much, throughout his life, about the great Prophet for whose sake, according to Muslim tradition, God had created the world, it was exciting to be present in the city of the Hejirah at his very tomb. Nabil felt very real and alive. People sat beside the tomb reciting the Qur'an; some would sit there for two or three days to recite the whole book over and over again. Crowds of people were shoving and pushing in an attempt to touch the tomb, which was covered with a golden curtain. Women wept, men threw money down on the floor beside the tomb - if only a person could touch the tomb, then all their sins would be forgiven!

Next to Muhammad's tomb were the tombs of the first two 'rightly guided' Caliphs - Abu-Bakr and 'Umar, considered to be the most excellent Muslims after Muhammad himself. Nabil and his uncle prayed at these tombs too before going for lunch in town. Uncle Muhammad was very hospitable and generous. Nabil stayed in his house and was treated as an honoured guest. He couldn't see his aunt, who spoke to him only through a closed door, welcoming him and asking about his family in Syria, and sending her greetings to them. His uncle was indeed very strict in his religious observance. Nabil had to accompany him five times a day for prayers at the Mosque. Over his four weeks' stay, this became a boring exercise, but there were some compensations for his uncle also took him sightseeing in and around Medina. He liked this city; it was an oasis, with many trees and water to be seen. In contrast, Mecca was dry and bare. They had some picnics, shopped, visited the school where his uncle taught and the mosque that Muhammad had built on his arrival in this city.

Uncle Muhammad would have liked Nabil to stay in Medina. He offered to arrange for him to study in the main Saudi Shari'a University, including arranging the special visa necessary to do this. But Nabil wouldn't hear of it. He was eager to leave the oppressive, stifling, religious atmosphere of Saudi Arabia and of his uncle's home to return to the relative freedom of Damascus University and his more easygoing friends. Saudi Arabia was also unbearably hot at this time of the year, and Nabil suffered from the heat. The Saudi people were very different to the Syrians. The people of Medina were mainly Beduins, some of whom had only recently settled in the towns, and there was not the sophisticated bourgeoisie Nabil was accustomed to in Syria. Even the richest of the Beduin were still rough desert nomads at heart and in behaviour, with the mindset of extreme Wahabi Islam. Nabil was impressed by the size of the country - the great Arabian Peninsula - and by the obvious efforts of the authorities to develop and modernize it. Some of the oil wealth was clearly being invested for the benefit of the country as a whole. This could be seen in the good roads and the many new buildings. On the other hand, in spite of their oil wealth, they still seemed bent on making as much money as possible out of the pilgrims. One had to pay for a visa, for official guides, for entrance to the holy sites, for sacrifices - and the larger part of this income went to the Saudi authorities.

After some forty days in Saudi Arabia, Nabil had done all that was expected of him. He was relieved to be free to return to Syria, to university and his friends. On his return he found himself treated as a celebrity. Family and friends crowded to see him, hug him, touch him, share the special blessing (baraka) attached to a Haji. He was supposed to be a new creation, without sin, a clean slate, like a newborn baby. For three days he just sat at home, talking to the visitors who came and went, telling them all about the Haj. How they all wished they could have gone! However, Nabil did not really enjoy all this attention. Also, traditionally he was expected to bring back mementos from the pilgrimage for his family - dates from the Holy City, holy Zemzem water, some holy sand - but Nabil hadn't bothered. His mother was very disappointed.

On return to university, Nabil was embarrassed by his friends who joked about his pilgrimage and called him a 'holy man'. 'Give us your blessing, Haj Nabil,' they would say, 'let us touch you and partake of your grace.'

It took a while for the excitement to die down. In the meantime Nabil's parents watched carefully to see if he had indeed changed. They soon noticed that the holy Haj hadn't made much difference to Nabil. Fairouz, especially, was very worried and spent much time talking to him about the importance of having the right attitude towards God and the religious requirements of Islam. She encouraged him not to neglect his prayers, to visit the mosque regularly, to read the Qur'an and to be a pious Muslim. 'Nabil,' she'd say, 'I hear the muezzin calling. Aren't you joining your father at the mosque for prayers?'

'Oh, I've just got to finish something I've started doing,' he would answer, 'I'll follow him to the mosque in a few moments.' But he would have no intention of going. Later he would invent excuses - he was too busy with his studies, so he had prayed alone in his room, he would say. There were many arguments and disagreements. It became a habit to deceive his parents in order to escape the constant pressure. The religious duties he did perform from time to time were simply not good enough for them. To be a really good Muslim, he had to do more - grow a beard, become a pupil of some famous Sheikh, study the Sunni Shafi'i school of thought and traditions, and read the prescribed commentaries.

The pressure to do more, upset Nabil. He considered himself a decent Muslim - after all, he believed, he prayed, he fasted, he gave to the poor, he had even gone on the Haj - why were they never satisfied? It was frustrating and he became very angry. Could they not just leave him alone? Surely they could not force him to do something he didn't want to do? He was determined to keep the basic rituals, if only they would leave him alone. Nabil believed in his own heart that religion was a personal matter.

University Days

Nabil was glad to be back at university and with his friends. His best friend, Kamal, also came from a good Sunni family; they had grown up in the same neighbourhood and had been together through primary and high schools. After his graduation Kamal emigrated to America. Ibrahim, a Palestinian, was another good friend who also lived in Nabil's neighbourhood. They had much fun together, but Hasib wouldn't allow this friendship to develop too far. Palestinians were considered 'different'; one was not supposed to mix with them. It was fine to support their cause against the Israelis, even to fight for them, if necessary, but otherwise one kept them at a distance. Hasib had refused several requests for marrying his daughters that had come from well-placed Palestinians. The Damascus Sunni elite looked down on Palestinians, as they did on so many other groups. The old tribal loyalties and taboos continued to be very powerful.

The university campus was set in the heart of Damascus, just behind the Exhibition Centre. Attractive buildings in the French colonial style were surrounded by well-kept grounds. A newer campus was later added for the humanities and arts faculties.

Sometimes, on his way home from university, Nabil would slip into a Christian church in order to observe their worship. One day, as he slipped furtively into the back rows of an Orthodox Church, his father's chauffeur, Joseph, saw him. Nabil was terrified. What if Joseph told his father? It would get him into endless trouble. He couldn't sleep that night and first thing the next morning phoned Joseph and begged him not to tell anyone. Joseph promised not to, and kept his word. 'But why did you do it?' Joseph asked Nabil.

'Oh, I just wanted to see how Christians pray; it was mere curiosity,' he replied.

Nabil was a rather introverted young man. Something always seemed to keep him from sharing his real feelings and innermost thoughts with his family. His father was too strict and distant; his mother treated him as if he was still a small boy. Anwar was too snobbish and too involved in religion, always pressurizing Nabil to join him in devotions. But Nabil hated the extremist environment Anwar moved in and it created a barrier between them. Only his middle sister, Amal, understood him. He felt at ease with her and could tell her some of his secrets, even about his romantic feelings towards some girl or his reflections on life. She always backed him up in times of conflict with Hasib.

Uncle Muhammad persuaded Hasib not to allow his girls to study at university. They had all finished high school and would have liked to go on into higher education. They pleaded and wept, they got Fairouz on their side to support their requests, but to no avail. University was seen as a potentially bad influence on them; it would expose them to the outside world, something no decent Muslim girl should be exposed to. So they had to stay home and wait until they got married - the earlier, the better.

Jamileh was the first to get married. Her husband was a young electrical engineer who was very religious and ran a study group in the local mosque. He had been one of Nabil's teachers. Amal, Nabil's favourite sister, got married to a businessman from a good family. They imported spare parts for cars. Though he was a good Muslim, Amal's husband was easygoing and tolerant, and he would often support Nabil and his lifestyle in a conflict with the more stringent demands of Hasib and Muhammad. Iman married a diplomat who worked at the presidential palace. From him Nabil learnt much about the inner workings of government, the intrigues and power struggles. He once arranged for the whole family to visit the Palace and have coffee there. It was an impressive occasion. Hasib was pleased with this son-in-law through whom he could extend his influential contacts.

Jamileh's husband tried to get Nabil involved in religious activities. This brother-in-law used to preach the Friday sermons in various mosques that did not have a qualified preacher. One Friday he invited Nabil along to a village mosque some distance from Damascus, to be the prayer leader and preacher. It was a small congregation of about twenty farmers. Nabil stood in front of them all and led the prayers. Then he went up to the pulpit to read the sermon his brother-in-law had written out for him. It was the first and the last time. He begged not to have to do it again. Nabil felt embarrassed; he was too shy.

Another time this same brother-in-law took Nabil to a Sufi (mystical Muslim) meeting held in the house of a very famous Islamic leader, Sheikh Hasan Habbannaki. Nabil had never attended anything like this before. They prayed and danced until they were in a trance-like state. Some people could not control themselves. One man in the centre of the crowd shouted sacred verses in a frenzy of weeping. Then he suddenly fell down in a fit, his limbs jerking. The onlookers attributed this to God's spirit who had entered him and put him in this special state of 'grace'. Most of the leaders who attended these meetings were in trouble with the authorities because of their extremist activities and were not allowed to leave Syria. When they wanted to go on the pilgrimage, they came to Hasib. He managed to arrange passports and permits for them and for their wives because of his position in the Ministry of Interior. It was no easy job and involved bending some rules, but Hasib felt it his duty to help these spiritual leaders in performing important religious rituals.

There was a lot of political activity in the university at that time; many groups were vying for influence and trying to recruit students to their ranks. The main confrontation was between the Muslim Brotherhood and the Ba'ath Party. Both groups invited Nabil and his friends to join, but Nabil was not interested. He was appalled at the violence used by the Brotherhood to attain their political goals. Many prominent people were assassinated, including a popular lecturer who was shot dead in his office by a student as he was preparing for a lecture, the only reason for the assassination given was the fact that the man was an 'Alawi. Many students were upset, but there was little they could do about it. Some students joined the Ba'ath party group, and they were later rewarded by being advanced very quickly to high positions in the Government.

Nabil worked hard at his studies. There were lots of seminars to attend, papers to hand in, exams to pass. It was a very busy time for him. Two hours a week were dedicated to military training - a new system recently introduced by the authorities. It was compulsory and meant that six months could later be deducted from a person's national service term. Nabil and some of his friends, still immature and spoilt youngsters, didn't take military matters very seriously and were in constant trouble with the officers in charge of the course. During the summer holidays they had to participate in a twenty-day basic training course during which they lived in tents, wore uniforms and had daily fitness drills. Nabil rebelled. He refused to eat the army rations or get up on time; he disobeyed orders. The officer was furious and sentenced him to solitary confinement under armed guard. He threatened to shave all his hair as well.

Hasib and Fairouz just happened to come and visit the camp at that time. Fairouz, who was always very concerned for her son in the harsh army surroundings, had prepared Nabil's favourite food and persuaded Hasib to drive her to the camp. Nabil was brought to the visitors' tent where he had to confess what had happened. Fairouz was shocked; Hasib was determined he should be left to learn his lesson. 'Oh no' , wailed Fairouz, 'we can't let them do this to him. You must speak to the officer.'

Hasib finally gave in and spoke to the commanding officer. He agreed to free Nabil on condition that he promised to obey orders and behave in an exemplary way for the rest of the course. Nabil, who was already planning to escape from this miserable situation (the penalty for that would have been a refusal to the next study year), readily agreed and rejoined the other soldiers. What a relief!

In the long summer holidays Anwar and Nabil worked for an uncle of theirs who had an agency for German office machines. It was good work experience, they earned some money and, most important of all, it kept them off the streets and out of trouble. Hasib insisted they had to take up these jobs instead of being idle.

Nabil enjoyed his student years. He was part of a group of around twenty boys and girls, all from good Sunni families, who did well in their studies and as a result were liked by the lecturers. Their main aim was to enjoy their university years together. Religion and politics were taboo for them; they preferred the cinema, discos and parties. They visited the Mediterranean and had picnics in the Ghuta oasis around Damascus.

Two girls, Rena and Iman, were especially fond of Nabil. They longed for him to ask their parents to marry them. But Nabil was enjoying the carefree bachelor life and felt he was far too young to contemplate marriage. Girls in Syrian society were under tremendous pressure to marry young and get settled as soon as possible. He felt sorry for these girls but, though he enjoyed their company, was certainly not in love with either of them.

Hasib and Fairouz were very keen to get their sons married to suitable girls as soon as possible. It was the custom for parents to arrange the marriages of their children. Fairouz spent over a year looking for the right girl for Anwar, carefully checking out families and their backgrounds. She wanted the perfect match - a good-looking, well-educated girl from a religious and wealthy Sunni family with a good reputation and easy to get on with as prospective relations. The women of the family would spend many hours discussing different girls, describing them in detail and comparing their virtues. Everyone in the extended family was involved in these discussions.

Finally Fairouz found the perfect match. The Muslim custom is to repeat a special prayer twice, just before falling asleep, asking God for guidance. Any memorable dreams that night are then assumed to be God's answer to the petition. Pleasant dreams meant 'yes'; but nightmares indicated a definite 'no'.

Grandmother, father, mother, uncles and aunts - all performed this ritual on the same night. The next morning they would report back. On this occasion everyone reported pleasant dreams - one had dreamt she was swimming in beautifully clear water, the other that he was walking high up in the mountains with a wonderful view all around him, the grass green, the sun shining - all were positive, and so they took it as confirmation from God and set about planning the marriage arrangements.

The couple was married just after Anwar graduated from university. They experienced quite a bit of marital trouble during their first year, as they had not known each other at all before their wedding. Then the extended family would get involved, to mediate, until they were more used to living together.

Once their eldest son was settled, it was Nabil's turn. 'Choose a girl. Get married. Give your parents the pleasure of seeing you settled down. Tell us if there is any particular girl you fancy.' Actually, his parents had already made a choice for him, namely a cousin who was five years younger, the daughter of Hasib's youngest brother. She was very pretty and had studied pharmacology. Her father had set up a pharmacy specifically for her; he had also bought her a house and a car. She was a very attractive proposition for any suitor. She and her mother would visit Fairouz almost every day. Hasib was greatly in favour of the match, because it was well-accepted in Muslim culture to marry a cousin; this strengthened family ties and kept accumulated wealth in the family. Fairouz too was in favour of this match and nagged Nabil about it every day. 'Nabil, this is the right girl for you. Just say "yes". You don't have to marry right now, but let us settle the arrangements.'

Nabil would not agree. He liked the girl, but she was more like a sister with whom he had played as a child. He couldn't imagine her as his wife, and was not ready to be tied down in marriage. He wanted to remain free for as long as possible. Though this caused many arguments and heated discussions, Nabil could not be persuaded.

Anwar became involved with the Muslim Brotherhood during his university years, although no one in the family knew it at that time. He continued to be a brilliant academic and, on graduation, was offered a teaching position at the University which he accepted. He wrote a textbook on civil engineering, which continues to be used till this day. Nabil helped with the typesetting and Hasib, the proud father, paid to have it published. It sold well and gave Anwar an early start in his business career. Anwar's final project was to design the foundations for the largest office building in Damascus. Nabil took a special course in technical drawing to be able to prepare the blueprints. The project was a great success.

However, the confrontation between the Government and the Muslim Brotherhood flared up again in 1980. Many of the Brotherhood were arrested, including Anwar's best friend (of whom nothing was heard subsequently). Hasib was very worried when he realized that his eldest son was involved in the Brotherhood. He knew that Anwar was in grave danger. A family council was called together and it was decided to help him flee the country as soon as possible. Fairouz recited the whole Qur'an in two days as penance for his ransom.

By using his position and connections, Hasib managed to get the Minister of Interior Affairs to grant a special permit for Anwar to leave Syria. Hasib had to pay $5,000 to the military authorities to have Anwar exempted from compulsory army service and then obtained a passport for him and put him on a plane to the United Arab Emirates. Everything happened so fast that there had been no time to get an entry visa to the UAE, but Hasib arranged for a friend to meet Anwar at Dubai Airport with a transit visa for seven days, which was subsequently extended. Anwar eventually settled in the UAE, where he started his own civil engineering and construction business. Some months later his wife joined him, flying out to Dubai accompanied by Fairouz.

Hasib was relieved when Anwar was safely out of Syria; from information in the Ministry of Interior he knew that the confrontation between the Government and the Muslim Brotherhood was bound to intensify in the struggle for power. Hasib's fears were fully justified when in 1982 the Brotherhood organized an uprising in the town of Hama, only to be brutally suppressed by the security forces with heavy artillery and tanks that levelled large parts of that old city. It is estimated that more than 20,000 people were killed in the confrontation. Thousands of the Brotherhood members and sympathizers all over Syria simply disappeared and were never heard of again.

Hasib had originally wanted both his boys to serve

in the Syrian Army, but Fairouz protested. She did not want the lives of her beloved sons endangered in the fighting in Lebanon, where the Syrian forces occasionally intervened in an effort to ensure Syrian hegemony over the divided land. She was also afraid that a war against their arch-enemy Israel could evolve out of the Lebanese debacle. No one believed that the Syrian army could win in an all-out confrontation with Israel.

As both the Government and the Army were controlled by the 'Alawis, the Sunni families did not feel morally obliged to send their sons for military service if they could avoid doing so. The 'Alawis were considered to be almost as much an enemy of true Islam as the Israelis were, and it was understood that they were consolidating their own power base under guise of a Holy War against Israel. So, why fight for them? It is a traditional rule of Islamic teaching that one should first fight the enemy who is the closest before attacking those who are further away. In the early 1980s Sunni religious leaders actually issued Fatwas that claimed it was as meritorious an act to kill an 'Alawi as it was to kill an Israeli.

The Sunni elite preferred to do the ruling; other groups could do the fighting! The very rich could avoid conscription by paying a sum of $5,000 as ransom for each son as well as sending their sons abroad for five years. After that period the young men could return to Syria legally without having to serve in the Army.

Having made the arrangement for Anwar to avoid conscription somewhat under pressure of events, Hasib and Fairouz decided to do the same for Nabil. On his graduation in 1982 they paid the $5,000 fine and put him on a plane to the UAE, this time with the necessary entry visa. Anwar met Nabil on his arrival and took him under his wing. He gave Nabil a job in his own company.

In the Arabian Gulf

Dubai town is the capital of the oil-rich emirate of Dubai, one of the seven emirates that constitute the United Arab Emirates of the Arabian Gulf. In the 1980s there was an economic boom due to the influx of oil revenues and people from all over the Arab world flocked to Dubai in search of well-paid employment. With a population of some 275,000 people at the time, amenities were thoroughly modernized and Dubai town, the largest city of the federation, became the economic capital, with road links to Abu-Dhabi and Ras al-Khaymah, two other important towns.

By the time Nabil arrived in Dubai, Anwar was well settled and successful in his business ventures. Nabil worked in Anwar's company for the first six months. He did some accounting and became a Jack-of-all-trades, turning his hand to whatever jobs were necessary. This was not a fulfilling or exciting existence.

After living with Anwar and his family for the first few weeks, Nabil rented a flat where he could have some privacy. He found it difficult working for his own brother, mixing family relationship with business, and he tried to get another job as soon as possible. A friend of Anwar's who ran a trading company needed an accountant, so Nabil was happy to accept that position and worked there for seven months.

Nabil soon noticed that the business of his new employer was going downhill and he decided to change jobs again. Anwar helped him by introducing him to another friend, this time a Syrian named Ahmad, who owned the large and flourishing Islamic Publishing House, which had branches in all the Arabic states and in many other countries. They published new editions of the Qur'an, Hadith, religious commentaries and reference books that were popular all over the Muslim world. Nabil was taken on as general manager of the firm's branch in Dubai. Soon his life there settled into a routine. The pay was good, he had a nice flat and, in order to enjoy better leisure facilities, he joined the exclusive Hyatt-Regency Hotel Club to have access to its swimming pool and sporting facilities. He went there daily with friends to swim, enjoy the sauna, play tennis, exercise - or play a game of chess, which was fast becoming a favourite hobby.

Ahmad liked Nabil. He would often ask Nabil to accompany him for lunch or dinner to some plush restaurant. Life was good and the future seemed promising. Occasionally Nabil would be sent abroad on business to Kuwait, Lebanon, Saudi Arabia, even Spain, Germany, France and Britain. Nabil enjoyed the travelling and it gave him a feeling of importance.

Once a year Nabil had to take his passport to the Syrian Embassy to have it stamped so that he would be allowed to return to Syria when five years were over. Hasib and Fairouz visited their sons twice a year, happy to see them doing so well. They knew Anwar could never return to Syria but looked forward to Nabil's return, at the end of the five-year period.

Nabil's friends in Dubai were mainly Syrians living in the oil-rich Gulf to make money. These Syrians were part of a large number of expatriate Arabs and other foreigners working in the UAE. Although they were never given citizenship, for the local people and Government were afraid these foreigners would take control of the economy, the Syrians were well respected as foreigners. They and the Lebanese were valued for their education and local people trusted them - Syrians were generally perceived to be competent and honest business partners. Jordanians were considered to be too much like the local Beduin tribes, people who did not like submitting to authority and preferred to be bosses giving the orders for others to obey! Egyptians were seen as weak and submissive, a legacy of their long history under the Pharaohs. Palestinians, who were viewed as politically dangerous troublemakers, were disliked although everyone was ready to fight for their cause.

The local UAE people were mainly first-generation city dwellers, of Beduin descent. They found young people like Nabil too westernized, not Islamic enough. They had strict rules about allowing other Arabs to work in their country, so that Anwar had to give a 51 per cent share of his company to a UAE citizen, whose sole contribution was that of contributing his name as co-owner. This man did no work and took no risks, yet earned $50,000 a year for the honour! As he could not even read or write, all he ever was expected to do was to fingerprint the contract that needed to be renewed annually.

The lowest class of society in the UAE was the immigrant workers from Pakistan, India and Bangladesh. They did the menial tasks that no one else wanted to do. Although they were Muslims they were treated scornfully, mere servants. They washed the cars, took clothes to the laundry, cleaned the flats and offices and swept the streets. Nabil found them very useful – he would pay one such a fellow to start up his car in the scorching heat so that the air-conditioning could begin to work. Then, after a few minutes Nabil could get into a cool car straight from his flat or office. These servants also brought Nabil tea or coffee at his desk; no task was too mean for them. They were paid for their services, but it was a paltry sum for the bad treatment they often had to endure. If a job was not done to his satisfaction, Anwar would think nothing of publicly slapping a servant across the face.

When hosting book exhibitions for the Publishing House, Nabil would employ the servants to do all the manual work of setting up the shelves and displays and cleaning the venue, while he and the other employees would wait around, drink coffee and chat until everything was ready. No one ever considered thanking these servants for their hard work.

However, Nabil discovered that these people were good, honest and humble. They were hard-working and loyal, and they never complained, argued or talked back like the Beduin often did. The servants would address their superiors, including Nabil, as 'Arbab', meaning 'Lord'. 'Yes, Arbab, okay Arbab, as you say, Arbab.' It was good for the ego of their employers, but it was a fact that these servants from the Indian subcontinent preferred to work for Syrians and other foreigners, who treated them less harshly than the local Arabs.

Nabil had two special friends in Dubai - Amir was an agronomist and a free thinker; Mu'in he had known from the mosque study group in Damascus. Both these men had left Syria, like Nabil, to evade military service. Each one tried to influence Nabil according to their lifestyle and world view. Amir took him out to enjoy the pleasures of life, while Mu'in would try to get him to go along to the mosque for prayers. Mu'in had established a study group in a local Dubai mosque, and Nabil sometimes went with him, mainly out of a habit of doing Islamic studies. In Dubai and all over the Gulf region, Islam is a strong social factor; everyone is expected to attend prayer times regularly. A person soon gets a good name if they are perceived to be an observant and pious Muslim; and this attracts business!

Nabil used much of his free time to read books. As he was in the publishing business, books were easily accessible and he soon he built up an impressive library in his flat. He read much about Islam, but also general reference works and science. He was a critical thinker who was always searching for answers, especially about the meaning of life.

His new independent lifestyle in Dubai made Nabil feel that he was maturing and developing his own personality for the first time in his life. He was completely on his own; no parents to fuss over him or control him; no one to dictate to him whom his friends should be or what he should be doing with his leisure time. He thoroughly enjoyed this freedom and concentrated his energies on developing his career. He improved business procedures in the firm, increased sales and contracted new clients. The Dubai branch of the Publishing House was flourishing under Nabil's leadership.

Yet, deep down in his heart Nabil felt uneasy. He had many questions, about religion and about life, for which he could find no answers. There was no one he could talk to about these things. Such topics were taboo; these were questions one dared not ask aloud; no one else seemed bothered by doubts or qualms.

People seemed satisfied with the old formulas given by traditional Islam, confident in their religion and focused on improving their material situation in the competitive economic climate of the Gulf; most people seemed oblivious to the many contradictions that Nabil noticed day after day and worried about.

The Discovery

Although Nabil had everything he could wish for materially, he felt an emptiness too, as if something was missing in his life. He often analysed himself to try and find the cause for this. What was wrong with him? After all, he believed in God, was moderately religious, attended the mosque and studied Islam. But God somehow seemed very remote and impersonal, an unknown force somewhere out there, beyond his grasp and comprehension. Was there a way to experience the presence of God more meaningfully?

Nabil remembered hearing Hasib talk to Fairouz about his religious life. He would say 'Look, Fairouz, I have done everything a good Muslim ought to do. I pray five times each day; I have been seven times on the Haj; I give the prescribed Zakat alms to the poor; I do all that God has commanded men to do – I do hope that God will accept me.' Hasib had a shaky hope that his deeds would merit him a place in Paradise, but he had no assurance of that. This bothered Nabil. Surely, when Hasib had done everything required of him, Paradise should be a guaranteed certainty? Why did he continue to fear the possibility of hell?

According to Islamic teaching only God knows what will happen in eternity to a person. God alone controls the final decision and no person can have assurance of their final fate. It appeared to Nabil that God could be very arbitrary, that no matter how hard you tried to win his favour, he could at the last moment decide to cast you into hell. As his will was supreme, one could never question his decrees, even if they seemed capricious. There were many traditional stories that illustrated just this, stories about evil people whom God decided to send to Paradise or good people whom he sent to hell. It all seemed so unfair and illogical. What kind of God was this?

Nabil realized that Hasib and other devout Muslims experienced God as a hard taskmaster, always waiting for them to slip up, to commit a sin so that he could pounce on them in judgement. They lived in constant fear of ending up in hell and worried much about it. Hasib used also to say to Fairouz, 'If I die, please don't forget to recite the Qur'an for me three or four times a year, and make sure you regularly visit the cemetery with my friends to pray for me.' These rituals were supposed to lift the soul of the deceased to a better place in the after-life, but could a person trust their family and friends to be faithful enough to perform these duties, year in and year out, after their departure? The chances seemed slim. It was all rather depressing.

Every day it was Nabil's duty to collect the firm's mail from the central post office in Dubai. One day he found a leaflet in Arabic, sent to the firm's address from somewhere in Lebanon. It was about the Prophet Issa (Jesus) and pointed out that he was actually a manifestation of God and the only way to happiness. Nabil read it before throwing it away thinking 'how stupid can you get'! From then on, every couple of months, a new leaflet or booklet would arrive. Sometimes it was mailed in Germany, sometimes in Lebanon and sometimes in Cyprus. He realized that this was illegal propaganda and that he should report it to the authorities, but something kept him back. He read every leaflet – how Issa was the Messiah who had died for the sins of mankind, how he loved all men and offered them free salvation. Nabil wasn't convinced by what he read. It was so different from his fundamental Muslim beliefs. Yes, Issa was a great Prophet, but he was only a man like all the other prophets. God can have no son; it is a grave sin to associate a man with God. Also, Issa didn't die; God caused someone else to die in his place and took him up to heaven. Nabil knew all the traditional Muslim arguments against Christianity and threw the leaflets away in disgust.

One of the leaflets offered more information and a free Bible if one wrote to an address in Cyprus. Nabil filled in the attached coupon and sent it off. He did want to know more. In spite of his prejudice, he enjoyed the new ideas; he was curious.

Some weeks later Nabil received the Bible, a small magazine called *The Key* and some more leaflets. He kept them all in his flat where he would read them in the evenings. The Bible was in modern, easy Arabic. Compared to the Qur'an it seemed rather flat and unexciting. No rhythm, no music, no lilt. It sounded like a normal secular book. Still, something compelled him to read on, although there was much that he could not understand.

Around that time Nabil met an American businessman, Henry Amherst, who represented several western publishers and sold scientific books to schools, universities and government offices. He used Nabil's book exhibitions for advertising his books and was a very good customer. Nabil sold him some of the Publishing House publications and slowly came to know him better. He liked this friendly, frank American who was scrupulously honest in all his business dealings. Soon they were solid friends. They would often meet over lunch or go to the beach for a swim. Then they would sip coffee and chat. They enjoyed each other's company. But Nabil's boss, Ahmad, was not happy with this friendship. He did not like westerners, especially not Americans, and he urged Nabil to limit his contacts with Henry to business matters only. Nabil resented this interference in his private affairs and it caused considerable friction between him and Ahmad.

Henry was married, but his wife and children lived in the United States. He would spend the cooler months of the year in Dubai and then take a long summer break of four months to be with his family in the States. Nabil liked Henry and admired his honesty, his readiness at all times to help anyone in need, his kind and thoughtful manner. Nabil had not come across such traits in his other friends and wondered what Henry's secret was.

Henry did much to help Nabil in his job. As he had worked in Dubai for many years he had many valuable contacts in business and government circles. He introduced Nabil to some of them and suggested others who might be interested in Islamic books. The Publishing House had just produced a very expensive edition of the Qur'an in a leather binding with gold lettering, a beautiful book, and Henry's contacts helped Nabil sell many copies of it.

One day Nabil casually mentioned that he had received a Bible and some Christian materials through the post. Henry didn't respond at the time but, later that week, he asked Nabil whether he was reading the Injil. Nabil told him that he was, but that he could not understand much of it. Then Henry told him about his faith as a Christian, how he sincerely believed that

Issa was divine and had died for his sins. He did not try and persuade Nabil, but from that time onwards they often talked about religion. Usually it was Nabil who would bring up the subject.

In typical Middle Eastern manner, Nabil often violently disagreed with what Henry said about Issa. But Henry always stayed cool and explained his beliefs in a logical manner. This impressed Nabil, who expected a slanging match. It was great to be able to talk to someone of another faith without getting upset when they disagreed or letting it destroy their friendship.

Then one day Henry asked Nabil if he would like to visit Henry at his home where a few friends would be meeting for prayer. Nabil thought, 'There is nothing wrong with prayer,' and agreed. At Henry's flat he met Henry's friends – they were all westerners. They drank coffee and chatted for a while before Henry asked people to share prayer requests. Then they started praying to God about these.

Nabil listened carefully. When they started 'Heavenly Father', he added 'Ya Rab' ('Oh Lord') under his breath. When they closed in Jesus' name he could see nothing wrong with it. After all Issa (Jesus) was a great Prophet and God was sure to answer prayers in the name of a Holy Man. What really struck Nabil was how informal and personal their prayer time was. They didn't recite formal prayers from a prayer book. They spoke their personal requests and needs to God as if they were addressing a kind, personal, caring father. God seemed very near to them, not far off and removed as in Islam. This was a totally new experience; it gave Nabil much food for thought.

Henry and his friends seemed such fine and

pleasant people. Nabil was attracted to them. At the same time it was as if a voice inside him was saying 'No Nabil, this is wrong; it is not for you, it is not Muslim.'

It was a confusing time for Nabil. He attended more of these prayer meetings, read the Bible and thought about the issues involved. There was so much he didn't understand, but Henry encouraged him to keep reading and praying for guidance. Reading through the Injil of Matta, some sayings of Issa stood out and challenged him in a special way by their moral force – 'But I tell you, love your enemies and pray for those who persecute you, that you may be sons of your Father in heaven' (Matthew 5:44,45). This was shocking! It was so opposed to all Nabil had learnt from his Muslim training. It caused a long and heated discussion with Henry. 'Look, Henry,' said Nabil, 'no one ever told me to love my enemies. We are taught to hate them and actively fight them. After all, that's what enemies are for. This is an impossible demand. I'll never be able to love an Israeli – they are enemies we are supposed to fight.'

'You're quite right Nabil,' answered Henry, 'it is very difficult, in fact it is impossible. Many things Issa asks us to do are beyond a natural person's power to perform. This is exactly why we need him and his power in our lives. This is why you need to believe in him.'

'Believing in him is easy,' said Nabil, 'we Muslims believe in him as a great prophet, we believe he was born of the virgin Maryam of God's spirit. But how can I accept him as God? God is one, unique, different, invisible, beyond human reach. I can never accept him as the son of God. That goes against all my upbringing and teaching.'

Another verse that Nabil noticed at this time was the one where Issa says 'It is not the healthy that need a doctor but the sick . . . For I have not come to call the righteous but sinners' (Matthew 9:12,13). This verse really amazed him when he first read it. 'Did Issa mean just the bodily sick?' he asked Henry, 'was he not interested in normal, healthy people?'

'Jesus means all of us,' explained Henry, 'we are all sick with sin. If you think that because you keep a few religious rules you are not a sinner, you are mistaken.'

Nabil was very touched by these revelations. Although he considered himself an honest man and a good Muslim, he was never really happy or relaxed, never completely at peace in his heart and mind. He was a loner, reading, thinking, avoiding society as much as possible, not enjoying the company of other people. He had always been a worrier and up till that point his religion had not helped him solve personal problems. When he read the words of Issa he felt something stirring within his soul, a hint of peace and fulfilment he had never felt before.

Nabil realized that to Henry and his friends God was near and personal, like a loving father whom they could trust, and to whom they could bring deeply personal requests for the ordinary things of life. This was a revelation. Prayer had always been a ritual to be performed in the prescribed manner, without asking why. God required it; that was enough reason to perform it. If people did not pray they could expect horrible punishments. Nabil had never experienced praying for personal needs or for the needs of others, but for Henry and his friends this seemed to be the most natural thing on earth.

They spoke about having a personal relationship with a God who loves people and accepts them as they are, a God who had forgiven all a person's sins because Issa had borne the punishment for them when he died on the cross. It was hard to believe – but a very attractive thought! Imagine not having to strain oneself to earn merit with God, able to relax and not worry whether one had kept all the requirements for that day, yet to have assurance that one's place in heaven is guaranteed – it seemed too good to be true.

Every night before falling asleep, Nabil would recite the Shahada thirty-three times with the help of a rosary. It was a deeply inculcated habit his mother had taught him as a little child. Should he die in his sleep, she used to assure him, he would be sure to die as a Muslim, not a Kaffir. No matter what sins he had committed during the day, that prayer made sure that he was a good Muslim for the night. Throughout those months of searching Nabil continued the habit, comforted by the knowledge that he still was a good Muslim.

Finally the time came for Henry's long summer holiday. Before he left he asked Nabil to keep an eye on his business and occasionally check his account books. Nabil was touched by such a display of trust. Henry also invited him to the USA, but Nabil wasn't planning a trip in that direction. He took Henry to the airport and on the way Henry advised him to go on reading the Injil even if he didn't understand it all. 'Just take it literally,' Henry said, 'don't try to read in between the lines.' He knew that in Islam a person is taught to read 'between the lines', to search for the hidden meaning behind the words of the Qur'an.

When Henry left it felt as if there was a gap in Nabil's life. He missed Henry. He didn't know what to do with himself in his free time, he had become so used to spending the time with Henry.

Several months later Nabil was due a long holiday. In a moment of sudden inspiration he decided to spend it in the USA! He would visit his old school-friend, Kamal, who was studying in Boston; maybe he would visit Henry too. It was much easier for a Syrian to get an American visa in the UAE than in Syria. The company was happy to pay half of his expenses.

Nabil flew from Dubai to JFK airport in New York. There he took a bus to Boston, where Kamal picked him up and took him to his flat. He stayed with Kamal and they enjoyed catching up on all that had happened during the years of separation. Nabil tried to contact Henry to arrange a visit, but Henry was away from home on business and the visit could not be fitted in.

One day a Lebanese Christian friend of Kamal's, Joseph, came to visit them. As they talked, Joseph told Nabil about his previous work. It involved visiting prisoners in the jails of Beirut to tell them about Jesus. Nabil was astonished. 'Those people got what they deserved for their crimes,' said Nabil, 'God arranged for them to get into jail, it is his will, they deserve their punishment, so why bother with them?'

'Oh no,' said Joseph, 'God still loves them and wants to save them. He has something more for them.'

'God definitely has nothing more for them,' answered Nabil, 'he is punishing them for their sins.' Joseph went on to speak rather disrespectfully of the prophet Muhammad. It infuriated Nabil and he almost lost control of himself; he could have hit Joseph when he insinuated that Muhammad was an insignificant man who had come from a disreputable family. 'Hold on,' shouted Nabil, 'you must be crazy. Everyone knows Muhammad came from the Quraish and they were the noblest family in Mecca. No Muslim will ever listen to your message if you distort the facts in this way.'

Some days later another Lebanese man and his son visited Kamal. With them came an American friend named Steve Mailer. As was customary in Arabic culture, they all sipped coffee and chatted. Nabil was impressed by Steve. He reminded him of Henry. Steve had worked for many years in a Muslim country and knew the social patterns and culture. He was soft-spoken, like Henry, and Nabil was pretty sure that he shared a similar belief. Before Steve left he arranged for Nabil to visit him the next day at his home in New Jersey.

The next day Kamal dropped Nabil off at Steve's place. They had a long conversation about religion. Nabil explained his situation, his spiritual search, the fact that he just could not go on living as he had been, torn between two faiths. He loved his family, his Muslim culture and society, but he had come to believe that Issa the Messiah was the only way to God. Steve explained that Issa was God, come in the flesh, who had offered himself as a perfect sacrifice on behalf of every undeserving sinner. Religious duties couldn't save anyone from being judged by a holy God. Every person needs a mediator who will reconcile them with God, and this mediator is Issa who, by his own death, obtained divine forgiveness for all who believe in him.

'Steve,' said Nabil, 'I really believe all you say; I want to become a true follower of Issa.'

'Not so fast, young man,' answered Steve, 'let's first pray about it and see how God guides us.' So they prayed together. Then Nabil returned to Kamal's home.

After forty-five days in the USA, he finally returned to Dubai. Sitting in the plane Nabil was still feeling pretty confused. Lost in thought, weeping inwardly, he prayed to God for guidance. 'I can't go on like this,' he said to God, 'I can't go on living a lie. I can't go with Anwar to the mosque or talk to my mother as if I was still a good Muslim, as if nothing had changed. I can't be a Muslim by day and pray to Issa by night. Please, show me what to do.'

Back in Dubai, Nabil was soon back into the old routine of work and leisure, but he had little peace. One night he just could not fall asleep. He went for a walk, knowing that he must face up to his situation. He could not live a double life. Walking through the dark streets, he finally made a clear decision. He believed in Issa, he believed that Issa had died for his sins; it was time to become a true follower of the Messiah.

It was a momentous decision that would totally change his life, though at that time he could not foresee just how difficult things would become for him. Having made the decision he felt happier than ever before; it was the happiest moment of his whole life. Nabil was completely at peace with himself and with God. He knew he had made the right choice!

Back in his flat Nabil recited the Shahada as usual before falling asleep. It was an old habit and died hard. It was as if he could hear a voice whispering 'If you don't do it and then don't wake up in the morning you will have died as a Kaffir.' It was several months before he managed to break this evening ritual.

When Henry arrived back in Dubai, Nabil happily

shared his decision with his friend. To his surprise Henry was not overjoyed. He felt Nabil was too much in a hurry. Basically he feared for his friend, knowing better than Nabil the grave consequences such a step holds for a Muslim in his own society. 'You have made a mistake,' he told Nabil, 'you can remain a Muslim and worship Issa at the same time. God will understand. If people find out about your decision it will be very tough for you.'

But Nabil was not convinced. In Islam you have to mention Muhammad and bless him and pray for him hundreds of times. You approach God on your own merits or through a sacrifice, not through a mediator who did it all for you. Islam prescribes that you have to deny that God can have a son. No, Nabil could not live as a Muslim and worship Issa.

Although Henry disagreed with Nabil's decision, he supported him solidly. He spent much time with Nabil in prayer and in reading and explaining the Injil to help him understand what it meant to be a true follower of Issa. Nabil enjoyed these times. However, when they moved from the Injil to the Old Testament, the Tawrah, Nabil was in for a shock. This was all about Israel, the arch-enemy of the Arabs! How could God have given them so many promises and privileges? Of course, in Islam it is recognized that God revealed the Tawrah and the Zabur to the Jews, and that Moses and other great prophets came from them. But they had disobeyed God and corrupted the scriptures, which was why God became angry with them and had punished them. God then sent his last messenger, Muhammad, with the final and true scriptures, the Qur'an, to the Arab peoples.

It was difficult for Nabil to accept that the Old Testament was a true account of God's dealings with humankind in the past and that the Qur'an's version was twisted. The whole tenor was so political, far too relevant to the modern-day Palestinian problem and all the emotions it arouses in Muslim Arabs. It took time for God to change Nabil's thinking. Finally he accepted that the whole Bible, from Genesis through to Revelation, was God's Holy Book.

Nabil noticed too that his character was changing or, rather, being changed, since he had become a believer in Issa. He now longed to spend time in prayer and reading the Bible. This was not like the compulsion of duty he had felt in Islam, but it was a joyful attraction. He did not have to look at his watch to see if it was time for prayers, for whenever it was his heart's desire to pray he could just talk to God – not because he had to, but because he wanted to. He was really happy; for the first time in his life the empty feelings of selfdoubt and meaninglessness were gone.

Nabil was still living in an Islamic country and working as manager of an Islamic publishing company. No one knew about his decision. He read and prayed in the evenings, in the privacy of his own flat, but never spoke to anyone about his new faith. He did not consciously change his behaviour, but Anwar and his boss noticed a change. They noticed that he neglected the mosque and once, when Ahmad visited him unexpectedly in his flat, he saw an Injil lying there. Anwar became very upset.

Things came to a head between Nabil and Anwar and Ahmad on the day of the terrible quarrel, which let to his dismissal without pay or compensation. It was good that Nabil had acted fast to get his military service status sorted out through the Syrian consul, because shortly after the quarrel Anwar phoned their parents in Damascus to tell them about the change he had noticed in Nabil. Their parents were extremely worried. Fairouz phoned Nabil several times to reassure herself that he was still a Muslim. 'Recite the Shahada for me,' she would then ask of him, 'I want to hear you saying it with my own ears.' Nabil obeyed, for he did not want to hurt her feelings.

'I heard you have become a Christian,' she would continue, 'is it true? Why do you have a Bible in your house, isn't the Qur'an good enough? If I ever hear that you have become a Christian, you will not be my son anymore; I will harden my heart towards you.' This is the most serious threat for any devout Muslim, because without their mother's or father's blessing they have no hope of getting to Paradise.

Fairouz was somewhat reassured when she heard Nabil say the words of the Shahada, but Hasib and Anwar were not so easily deceived. Hasib did not get in touch with Nabil personally; he used Anwar as a go-between to express his disapproval and shock. Nabil was hurt by his father's hardness . . .

These were the things Nabil remembered as he settled down in his seat on the aeroplane heading for Poland. He fastened his seatbelt; it was a relief, at last, to be getting away from it all.

Romance in Poland

During his work for the Islamic Publishing House, Nabil had flown to various countries to help coordinate the special luxury edition of the Qur'an which they were producing. This was a large and complicated project that took meticulous attention to details. A single error in a Qur'an means the whole print run will have to be destroyed. The book had to be perfect down to the smallest vowel mark.

As Aḥmad could not speak English he delegated to Nabil the job of dealing with their English-speaking partners in non-Arabic-speaking countries. It meant Nabil had to travel to Lebanon, Spain, France, Germany and India to coordinate the project.

On one of his trips to Europe Nabil and his colleague had to spend several days in Warsaw while waiting for a connecting flight. Nabil's companion suggested that, instead of waiting near the airport, they take the train to Cracow and visit his cousin, who was studying there. Nabil agreed. The cousin invited them to a party he was attending that evening. They gladly accepted. At the party Nabil was introduced to a young Polish woman named Renata. She was a striking girl, tall and dark with laughter in her eyes. Nabil was in love at first sight!

This was the same Nabil who had resisted the idea of marriage for years despite the constant pressure from his mother who, every time she visited him in Dubai, would bring fresh news of suitable girls who were interested in him. Meeting Renata, changed all that. His defences were down and he could think of nothing but her. She seemed to feel equally attracted to him – after all, he was a good-looking, mysterious stranger from the fabulously rich Arabian Gulf. They talked about themselves and their jobs (Renata was a senior secretary in offices of the local Town Council), and Nabil lost no time – he invited her out to dinner the very next day.

The next evening Nabil and Renata had a romantic dinner together and afterwards Renata showed him some of the favourite sights of her city. In true Arab fashion he proposed marriage there and then. Renata was somewhat taken aback – were things not moving too fast? She did think she loved him, but needed time to consider it all. So they agreed on a trial engagement, which would leave them both space to reflect on their true feelings while getting to know each other better.

Renata introduced Nabil to her mother and to her colleagues at work. They all liked him. Everyone exchanged addresses and, on his return to Dubai, Nabil and Renata continued to keep in touch through regular correspondence and frequent phone calls.

Nabil now spent his holidays in Poland. It did not take long for them both to feel ready to consider marriage. They started the official application for the necessary permits, but soon found themselves in the centre of a very unusual situation. Nabil and Renata were both inexpressibly naive about life. They knew hardly anything about each other's background and culture or the intricate political and legal maze they were letting themselves in for. They knew only their love for each other and were certain that was strong enough to overcome all obstacles.

Renata came from a large, traditionally devout Roman Catholic family. The family members were close and spent much time together. Although her family all liked Nabil and could see that he was 'a good man', like many people who live in small and isolated communities, they distrusted foreigners. 'He's a Muslim,' they would say to Renata, 'he most likely has other wives out there in the Gulf; he can divorce you any time he wishes, take care!'

Nabil and Renata communicated in a most amazing way. Renata spoke a little English, which she had learnt at school but never used before, and she certainly knew no Arabic. At first they had to enlist the help of friends, who acted as interpreters, but soon they invented their own code of sign language. However, Nabil was determined to learn Polish and threw himself into it with such enthusiasm that it was not long before he was able to communicate in a simple way. At the same time Renata was working hard at improving her English – a slow process.

Nabil did try to explain to Renata something of his new faith in Jesus, but communication was difficult and, although she was happy to hear that he, a Muslim, believed in Jesus, she was sure he must have been taken in by some dangerous sect such as the Jehovah's Witnesses, a taboo to sincere Catholics. For Renata and her family the Roman Catholic Church was the only true Christian Church, the only source of true faith and salvation. How could he, a Muslim, know anything about being a Christian, Renata and her family wondered. They tried explaining some of their doctrines to him, but to no avail. Nabil found it confusing when he was confronted with the divisions within Christianity, but he remembered Henry's and Steve's advice to stick to the Bible as the ultimate authority for his faith. He could see that some of the Catholic rites had little to do with the teaching of the Bible. He also continued to keep in touch with his two American Christian friends by phone and by letter. They advised him not to push his faith on Renata, but to let God work out things in his own time.

Nabil had tried to keep his relationship with Renata a secret from his family. However, a short while after he had first met her a Syrian friend, who had been living in Dubai and who knew all about their relationship, returned to Syria and visited Hasib and Fairouz. He told them what he knew about Nabil's romance as well as his interest in the Christian religion. What upset them was not that Nabil wanted to marry a Christian woman, which is allowed by Islamic law, but the fear that any children born to Nabil, their own grandchildren bearing the Madani family name, might be brought up as Christians rather than as Muslims. This thought upset them and it was made worse by their suspicion that Nabil was seriously interested in Christianity.

Nabil wrote them a short letter to explain his situation. He enclosed a photo of Renata. His parents responded in a cool way. As far as they were concerned, she was much too old for him (actually she was three years younger than Nabil, but in Arab culture a five-year age difference or more is preferable). His parents considered it a foolish relationship. After all, he could marry a girl from any of the most respectable families in Syria, so why should he prefer a foreigner who was also a Christian? Hasib and Fairouz tried hard to entice him back to Damascus. They promised to arrange a marriage to any Syrian girl he liked if only he would return, but

Nabil refused. He was afraid of his father's harsh manner and of the constant supervision he would be under if he ever went back to his family. Furthermore, he had made up his mind to marry Renata, come what may! When his parents understood how determined he was, they tried to get him to convert her to Islam. If she converted they would be happy to accept her as their daughter-in-law; Nabil and Renata would even be welcome to live with them. They were willing to do anything to ensure their grandchildren would be raised as Muslims.

The procedures to get the marriage approved took eighteen months. The Syrian authorities required a multitude of forms and papers. In order to ascertain whether Renata had any Jewish relations, she had to provide her ancestral genealogy for several generations back, and have it all translated into Arabic. These had to be sent to Damascus for approval, and then back to Warsaw. It was a bureaucratic nightmare! Finally Nabil took recourse to his father's old trick – using people with influence. He had a friend from high school days who lived in Damascus and who was friendly with one of the President's sons. Nabil begged him to do something, for he could see no way out of the bureaucratic maze. The friend kindly obliged and mentioned Nabil's case to the President's son, who phoned someone in the appropriate Ministry and, hey presto, everything was miraculously approved!

Hasib knew nothing about this contact of Nabil. When he later heard about it, he was so upset that he cut off all relationships with that young man. Hasib had sincerely hoped the permits would never be allowed, that Nabil would return to his senses and give up his Christian fiancé.

Nabil and Renata finally received the necessary permits from both the Polish and the Syrian authorities. They were married at a civil ceremony in Cracow in February of 1986. Nabil stayed in Poland for two months before returning to Dubai to continue his work. Then in December 1986 the quarrel with Ahmad and Anwar took place. Until then Nabil had believed it would be possible for his family to accept his chosen lifestyle and for him and his wife to settle in the Middle East. But when he was ordered to leave his employment it indicated to him that he had to make a choice; the time had come to break with the culture of his childhood. He left Dubai to join his young Polish wife in Cracow just in time for the birth of their first son Piotr.

Nabil had hoped he would be able to start a new life in Poland, to get a job and settle down. But, his hopes were soon dashed when it became clear that there was no chance of his being granted a residency permit. As a tourist he had to exchange $15 a day at the official exchange rate - it was worth much more on the black market – and, in addition, had to renew his visa every month. He was not allowed any waged employment and, as a result, his savings were fast dwindling. He tried every solution he could think of - but to no avail. In desperation he contacted the Syrian Embassy in Warsaw and asked them to put pressure on the Polish immigration authorities on his behalf, but they refused. The Syrian consul told him that under no circumstances would they interfere in an internal Polish matter – the best thing for Nabil to do was to return to Damascus!

After six months in Poland when Nabil went to the

Polish Immigration Office to ask for the regular monthly extension of his tourist visa, it was refused. There was nothing to gain from pointing out that Nabil was married to a Polish woman - the administrator was adamant that he had to leave Poland. He suggested Nabil leave and try to re-enter from abroad. Nabil thought this was just stubbornness by a junior official and tried to contact someone with more influence in the Polish Ministry of Interior but, again and again, the message was the same: if Nabil did not leave of his own free will, he would be deported.

During these harrowing days Renata was struck by Nabil's steadfast personal faith in Jesus. He spent much time in prayer and she was touched by the sincerity and simplicity of these prayers. No ritual, no formulas – he just poured out his heart to Jesus. She could not understand why he did not make the sign of the cross before he prayed, or recite the 'Hail Mary'. She was even more surprised that he as a lay person read the Bible on his own – she had come to accept this as something only priests could do.

Nabil and Renata finally capitulated to the pressure from the authorities. As there was no other option open to them, they decided to fly together to Damascus to see what they could achieve in the Syrian capital. Piotr was just four months old when they left Poland and Renata was newly pregnant with her second child. She had never been to the Middle East before. She also knew Nabil's family had rejected them both and may have set things in motion to 'rescue' their grandchildren, but she was determined that she would not desert Nabil; she and Nabil would stick together through thick and thin.

Exiles

Nabil was very worried that his family might hear of their arrival in Damascus. He had kept in touch with his favourite sister Amal and had heard that Anwar had turned Hasib and Fairouz against him, claiming that he had converted to Christianity and was now a renegade Muslim who deserved to be killed, in accordance with Islamic law. Anwar and his Uncle Muhammad had even urged Hasib to contact Nabil, give him a few days to recant and, if he should refuse to, to fulfil the law by arranging for him to be killed in one way or another. Fairouz had strongly objected, pleading that they leave Nabil alone as long as he remained abroad, to which they reluctantly agreed.

Hasib, however, was furious. Nabil had brought shame on the family name and had deeply wounded his father's pride; he had turned his back on everything Hasib valued in life. Hasib felt he had become the laughing stock of his friends and he was ashamed to face his colleagues at the Ministry. He solemnly declared before all family members that he no longer considered Nabil to be his son, that he had removed his name from his will and that he would try to kidnap Nabil's children if ever there was an opportunity, in order to bring them up as real Muslims. The family members were warned to cut off all contact with Nabil or face their father's ire.

Nabil and Renata had not told anyone of their flight to Damascus in an effort to keep it a secret from Nabil's family. Renata was frantic at the thought that they might take Piotr away from her. She would have liked to meet her in-laws, but was too afraid on Piotr's account. She knew that Hasib, as the grandfather, could legally detain his grandson in Syria, claiming that his son had apostatized from Islam. Piotr was on her Polish passport and not on Nabil's Syrian one in case she had to leave quickly on her own. On arrival in Damascus they took a taxi to the Christian quarter where they rented a room in a convent, which also served as a hostel.

Nabil and Renata tried at the various embassies in Damascus to get visas to a western country, but without success. Finally they went to the Cypriot Embassy. Here the consul was very friendly and sympathetic. He listened to their story and then decided to give them a ten-day visa for Cyprus, although Renata was supposed to have applied for it from Warsaw. He also gave them a letter to the Cypriot immigration authorities to explain their predicament and advised them to apply for political asylum once they arrived in Cyprus.

They now needed exit visas from Syria, so they approached the Syrian Ministry of Interior with some trepidation. The official asked them to fill in three separate forms. Nabil had to provide a permit from the Ministry of Defence, and he had to give his written approval for his wife and son to receive an exit visa. It was all very complicated; Renata was so nervous she burst into tears at one point. Finally all passports were stamped and they could leave the building with a feeling of relief. Nabil had been afraid of meeting someone who knew his father.

Six weeks after arrival in Damascus everything was finally ready for their flight to Larnaca in Cyprus. At the airport check-in counter their luggage was found to be overweight and they were asked to pay a large sum for it. Being very short of money, Nabil looked for a friend of his uncle who worked at the airport to ask for his help. This man spoke to the airline officials and they let the luggage through without further trouble. However he also insisted on telling Nabil's family that he had seen him - he apparently knew nothing of their problem.

Nabil later heard from Amal that this friend had phoned Hasib, and that Hasib had been furious. He called the family together again to assure them that he would not have let Nabil and Piotr leave Syria, had he known they were in Damascus. He would have had their passports cancelled and would have turned Piotr into a good Muslim. He repeated that Nabil was now no longer his son; anyone who dared mention his name again would be disinherited, just as Nabil was.

On arrival in Cyprus the young couple rented a small flat in Limassol. From there Nabil phoned Amal, who told him how outraged Anwar and Uncle Muhammad had been at not having caught him and his family in Damascus. They were making plans to trace him in Cyprus, so that they could send an emissary to give him the customary three days to recant as required by Shari'a law. If he failed, they would have him killed. Hasib seemed to have approved this plan, but Fairouz was fiercely opposed to it and threatened that she would leave Hasib if he should act upon it. 'He is not our son anymore,' Hasib shrugged, 'so let him be.' And so the wild plans for revenge were abandoned.

But Hasib could not ever forget Nabil's defection; he vowed that he would yet get both Nabil and Piotr back to Islam. He charged Anwar to kidnap the children. To Fairouz he said, 'How can I face my colleagues at work after all this? They all know that my son is a Christian – it is a great shame on our family honour. I gave him everything and this is how he repaid me, his father.'

When Amal related all this to Nabil on the phone, it saddened him. He understood his father's dilemma; he still loved his parents. He knew the terrible prejudice and misconceptions they had about Christians and Christianity. Only God could change these hardened attitudes. Nabil knew it was better for him to cut off all communications with them, for the sake of his family's safety.

The next time he phoned Amal she asked him to be brief. Her husband was giving her trouble because of her contact with Nabil; he had forbidden her to have any contact with Nabil by phone or in writing and had warned her that he would divorce her if she dared disobey. Nabil was sad to sever that last link with his family.

Nine days after arrival in Cyprus they went to the immigration officer in Limassol with all their documents, hoping to extend their visas. The uniformed officer was a large man with a bushy moustache. He reminded Nabil of his own father. Having looked at their passports, he read the letter from the consul in Damascus and immediately jumped up in rage. 'No way,' he exclaimed, 'we are a peaceful country in a very delicate situation. We have just had a civil war between Christians and Muslims. We don't want any trouble with Syria.'

Nabil explained that he couldn't return to Syria, but the officer was adamant that he had to leave Cyprus immediately when his visa expired. Nabil's American friend, Steve, had given them the address of a Lebanese believer who lived in Limassol. Nabil now went to see this man, Edward, who introduced him to another Christian believer, Richard. Richard was an American and he accompanied Nabil back to the Immigration Office to beg them to grant the Madanis an extension on humanitarian grounds. The stern officer agreed to give them another ten days if they could put up a cash guarantee of £600. Richard took Nabil back to his own home, told him to wait there and slipped out to his bank. He soon returned with the required amount of money. Nabil was very astonished that this complete stranger was willing to give him such a large amount of money on trust!

At the Immigration Office the official could hardly believe his eyes when Nabil rushed in with the required amount. They had ten days' extension!

What to do next? This was the big question. Richard, who worked in Cyprus as a translator for an overseas company, spoke fluent Arabic and turned out to be very helpful. He had many contacts and started phoning around to see what could be done. Someone suggested they see the Greek Orthodox Bishop of Limassol and ask for his help. They obtained an audience for the next day and Richard accompanied them there. The Bishop's residence was a very impressive place, and on meeting him they had to kiss his hand, according to approved protocol. He was very friendly and listened to their story most sympathetically. He immediately sat down to write a letter to the chief immigration officer in Limassol to ask him to grant the Madani family residence in Cyprus, even if it broke all the accepted rules! The Madanis left with their hopes raised.

As a result of this letter, they were granted forty-five days' extension on condition that someone in

Cyprus guaranteed to cover all their costs, including health expenses if necessary. Richard again proved a true friend. The immigration officer could not believe his eyes when Nabil returned the next day with all the required letters. He had tried getting them out of the country; now they were set to stay on for sixty-five days. They seemed to have helpers and friends all over the place - the official had never seen anything like this before. He was all the more sure now that they were part of some sinister political plot and assured them this was the very last extension he would grant them.

Nabil wasn't allowed to work in Cyprus. Their funds were getting low. Through Amal he had tried to get Anwar to transfer some of the outstanding money owed him by his former boss and from the sale of his car in Dubai, but Anwar would do nothing of the sort. He refused to help Nabil in any way, unless he first repented and apologized, saying Nabil deserved all the troubles he now had.

Richard, however, continued to encourage Nabil. He visited the various western embassies to see if any one would allow the Madanis to immigrate, but for some reason a mixed marriage between a Syrian and a Pole proved an obstacle to them all! Finally Nabil approached the Red Cross for asylum-seeker status on the grounds of religious persecution. The lady in the office was sympathetic, but their case had to be referred back to the Red Cross headquarters in Geneva; it would take time before they could give their verdict.

'What about their residence status in Cyprus in the meantime?' asked Richard who had again accompanied Nabil to this interview.

'That's okay,' said the lady from the Red Cross, 'as

soon as we accept someone's application for asylum, the Immigration Office has to grant them a residence permit until we get the final verdict.' She gave Nabil an official letter for the immigration officer.

The same man with the large moustache who had first received them, was very upset to see them in front of his desk again. 'You are dishonest,' he accused them, 'you are playing tricks on me.' However, he had no choice but to grant them an open-ended extension, awaiting a decision from the Red Cross organization.

Three months passed without any progress on the visa front. Then Nabil was contacted by the Red Cross office and the lady who first interviewed them told them that, sadly, the Red Cross Headquarters in Geneva had refused their application. Nabil was devastated. 'But why did they refuse it?' asked his friend Richard.

'They classified this case as an internal domestic problem,' she answered, ' they won't deal with it. They only deal with cases of official persecution by the ruling government. Can you provide proof that that is what is happening to you?'

'No, I can't,' said Nabil, 'I left Syria legally. The Government was not involved; it was my own choice to leave; my own family caused my troubles.'

'Did they threaten you in any way?' asked the official.

'Yes they did,' replied Nabil, ' my sister told me that my father had decided I was a Kaffir and that Islamic law needed to be applied to me. That means death.'

'Do you have that in writing?' she asked.

'No, this was conveyed to me by phone.'

'Can't you ask your father to put it in writing?' she persisted.

Nabil laughed. This was too ridiculous! Ask his father to oblige and write him a threatening letter, just so that the Red Cross could help him! What kind of a world did these people live in?

'We must have written proof,' the lady continued sympathetically, 'why don't you write a letter as if it came from him and sign it yourself? No one in Geneva would notice the difference.' She was trying her best to help them.

Richard and Nabil looked at each other, then shook their heads.

'Thank you, no,' they said, 'we can't do that, even if it would help.'

She looked at them, clearly frustrated. 'I'm very sorry, I only want to help you. We must have written proof.'

It seemed the end of this thread. The lady promised to delay replying to the Immigration Office about them for ten days, just in case something turned up. She wished them well and saw them to the door.

Two weeks later Nabil received a letter from the Cypriot Immigration Office: 'Dear Mr. Madani, the Red Cross has informed us that your application for asylum has been refused. You are requested to leave Cyprus within 48 hours.'

Renata was now four months pregnant. Suddenly Richard had a brainwave. 'I wonder if women who are pregnant are allowed to fly?' he mused. 'I know a doctor at the local hospital, let's ask him, he might know.'

Richard phoned his friend who advised them that, according to Cypriot law, a woman more than three months into her pregnancy was not allowed to fly! He offered to write a letter to the authorities to point this out. Richard and Nabil drove over to the hospital, picked up the letter and, armed with this new bit of authority, marched confidently up to their old friend with the big moustache at the Immigration Office.

'Mrs. Madani can't fly out of Cyprus because she is four months pregnant,' they told him, 'here is the medical document to certify that.'

This time the official almost exploded. He jumped off his chair and swore at them in Greek. 'Mr. Madani must leave,' he shouted at them, 'Mrs. Madani can stay until she's had the baby.'

'I'm sorry you take this case so personally,' said Richard softly, 'I suggest the case be referred to the main office in Nicosia.'

The officer seemed relieved. He threw the file at them. They went out and straightaway called a taxi to take them to Nicosia, where they saw the top official in charge of immigration matters. They also took a Cypriot solicitor with them, a friend of Richard. The official studied the file and seemed quite friendly. Finally he picked up the phone and called the Limassol office. 'Mr. Kololombo,' he said to their old friend, 'I am sending Mr. Madani back to you. You must extend his visa indefinitely until his wife has given birth.'

Mr. Kololombo must have had a near heart attack when he received this order. But there was nothing he could do about it. To be spiteful he insisted that they get a medical certificate from a government-employed doctor, which their friend at the hospital speedily arranged. Their passports were duly stamped and, for the first time since arrival in Cyprus, Nabil and Renata could relax – they could look forward to more than five months free of visa problems. It was wonderful not to have imminent deportation hanging over their heads.

Struggling
in Limassol

The fear of deportation was gone for the moment, but there were other problems. Nabil and Renata had very little money left. Cyprus was an expensive country to live in. They had to pay rent and utilities and there was little left for food. They struggled to afford buying bread and milk for Piotr. As a last resort they started walking the beaches at night to collect empty bottles, thrown away by the tourists – Pepsi bottles, beer bottles, whatever. Armed with plastic bags they would comb the beach every night and collect as many bottles as they could find. Then they would take them home, wash them and then sell them at a collection point. They got approximately 1p per bottle! If they managed to collect 100 bottles, they had enough money for a loaf of bread and some milk.

They also had some health problems, but no money to pay for a visit to the doctor. Piotr was suffering from malnutrition; Renata was pregnant and could have benefited from a more balanced diet and regular medical check-ups; Nabil had a bad tooth which bothered him so much that he finally extracted it himself – a painful operation which left him suffering from an infection in the root canal.

Renata was very supportive of Nabil during all this time. She could have left him and travelled by ferry and train back to Poland with Piotr, but she didn't even consider it. Although she wasn't happy with Nabil's beliefs and didn't understand all the bureaucratic jumble they faced, she considered it her duty to stay with her husband. This touched Nabil deeply.

During their first months in Limassol, Richard and Edward had introduced them to a group of Christian believers who met regularly in various homes for prayer and Bible study. Nabil loved going there, but Renata refused. She was still a staunch Catholic and asked Nabil to find her a Catholic Church she could attend. He faithfully walked around the streets of Limassol looking between the many Greek Orthodox churches until he finally located a small Catholic Church. Renata was happy and attended there regularly.

Of course Nabil and Renata did have arguments and disagreements during this time of living with such pressure and uncertainty. At times they talked about divorce; it seemed an easy option, but by God's grace they always found their way back to each other to struggle on together. Nabil found peace in his prayer times when he could talk quietly to his heavenly Father, assured that he was present. Prayer became his lifeline as all material support apparently disappeared and he realized how totally dependent he was on God for everything. Direct answers to his prayers strengthened his faith and helped him to trust God even more.

His friends at the Christian fellowship group were also very supportive – but he was too proud to tell them the truth about his desperate financial situation. He couldn't beg! He had been brought up in a middle-class family; never before did he have to beg or look for help to meet his physical needs. To ask for help went against his grain; Nabil just did not know how to cope with such a situation. However, God was teaching him some basic lessons in humility.

Renata was different. She had been brought up under Communist rule. Provisions had always been scarce; since childhood she learnt to make the most of every scrap. She could barter in the market for the cheapest goods and was not averse to picking up useful things, even from rubbish bins, that were discarded by richer people. In this way she found some excellent toys in good working order for Piotr.

One day Edward, their good friend from the fellowship group, visited them at home in their flat. 'Is everything okay, Nabil?' he asked, 'is there anything you need?'

'No, no,' said Nabil, too proud to admit their need, 'everything is fine.'

At that point Renata burst into tears. 'He's lying,' she told Edward, and went on to explain to him their real situation.

Edward was astonished. 'Nabil,' he said, 'this is not right. This isn't the way a believer behaves. Don't be too proud to accept help from others.' Being Lebanese himself, he did understand Nabil's behaviour to some extent, but his western friends could not understand it at all. From that day on they always approached Renata with their offers of help, and things certainly did improve for the Madanis.

Edward was a good friend. Nabil would often visit him in the evening after working hours. They would sit on the roof of Edward's house and talk about the Bible or spend time together in prayer. Nabil had so many questions about his new faith, and Edward was very patient in trying to answer them to the best of his ability. Nabil's understanding of the Bible grew tremendously through these quiet conversations with his friend.

Edward also provided them with a TV set and suggested they watch Middle East Television from Lebanon, a Christian station broadcasting in Arabic. Nabil loved the daily messages. After every sermon the preacher would invite his audience to join him in prayer, and Nabil would kneel down at the sofa in their living room to join the prayer time – a wonderful source of encouragement and teaching during these difficult days.

At the Christian fellowship group, many prayed for Renata to come to a personal faith in Jesus. During the first months in Limassol she would not go near this group, adamant that she wanted Piotr to be brought up as a good Catholic. There were times when she even forbade Nabil to read his Bible at home. However, she did also realize how much he was willing to suffer for his faith. One day she said 'This is really stupid! Why suffer so much? Just go back to Islam. Let's return to Syria to lead a normal life; we can't struggle on like this forever.' But on another evening she surprised Nabil by announcing that she was joining him to go to the fellowship meeting that evening. 'Roberta, Edward's wife, invited me to come,' she explained, 'I'll just drink coffee with you all, but don't expect me to participate!'

At the meeting Renata sat quietly through the study and listened intently to all that was said. She joined Nabil again for the following two studies and, after the second one, asked Edward into the kitchen for a talk. She wept as she told him that she now wanted to believe like Nabil. What should she do? How should she go about it? Edward assured her that there was nothing to do; she simply had to believe in Jesus and all that he had done for her. There was no rite, no ceremony. Edward prayed with her and she joyfully accepted Jesus into her life.

Back home that evening she cried and apologized to Nabil for her former critical attitude to his faith. It was a tremendous change. How wonderful now to be united as a couple in their love for Jesus. Renata started attending the Bible studies regularly and set about praying and reading the Bible on her own. Talking about their faith now became a source of great mutual encouragement.

Through Richard, Nabil was put in touch with a company who needed an Arabic editor to check the scientific publications they had translated from English into Arabic. The company supplied him with a word-processor so that he could work from his own home. During the day he helped Renata with the housework; at night he worked on the manuscripts. The publishing company was very pleased with his work and paid him secretly. Next they wanted to employ him officially, so they applied to the Cypriot Ministry of Interior for a work permit for Nabil. The response was negative. The company assigned a solicitor to the matter, but still their request was refused. The reason given was that the Madanis, on arrival in Cyprus, had applied for political asylum (as suggested to them by the Cypriot consul in Damascus). This had obviously been a mistake and the authorities now used it to refuse them residency status and work permits in Cyprus. It was extremely frustrating.

It was especially frustrating as there were so many Arab refugees in Cyprus – mainly Lebanese and Palestinians. They all seemed to have no problem sorting out their immigration status and finding work in Cyprus, but for some reason the authorities consistently refused it to the Madanis. They were apparently afraid of repercussions from the Syrian Government.

During the months that followed, Nabil visited all the western embassies in Cyprus in turn to look for an opportunity to immigrate – Canada, USA, Australia, Germany. Each in turn said that he was free to apply, but that the application would need to be referred back to his home country for approval and that it could involve a long process. No one could offer him protection from the Cypriot authorities if they asked him to leave while his application was being processed. The Madanis filled out innumerable application forms, but all came to nothing. Syrians, at that time, were simply not welcome anywhere in the West because of the Syrian connection with militant terrorist groups. It seemed a hopeless situation.

At the fellowship meetings Nabil also met Grant and Edith, an English couple working for a Christian organization in Cyprus. Nabil immediately felt attracted to them - there was something special about them and they cared very much about his difficult situation. Grant promised to contact his organization, which had branches all over the world, to see if there was a vacancy for a trained accountant anywhere. Alternatively, Grant suggested, they could enroll as participants in the organization's one-year training programme, which some western governments recognized as a valid endorsement for granting visas to applicants from non-European countries.

Only weeks later Grant heard that the English office indeed needed an accountant and would be happy to apply for Nabil and his family to join them in Britain for one year as members of their training programme. The Madanis would have to apply for this one-year visa in Cyprus; the office in the UK would then back their application by certifying to the Home Office that they had been accepted for the organization's training programme.

Nabil, Renata and Piotr, accompanied by the faithful Richard, set off for the British Embassy, this time with a glimmer of hope. Would it be the answer to their prayers, would this door finally open for them? The British consul was quite friendly. He first interviewed Renata on her own for half-an-hour, although her English was still rather weak. Then he spoke to Nabil, 'As you know, there are no diplomatic relations between our countries.' (It was shortly after the case of Hindawi, who had tried to blow up an Israeli passenger plane in Britain on behalf of the Syrian secret service; as a result Britain had broken off diplomatic ties with Syria.) 'I advise you to go to Damascus and apply from there. How long have you been in Cyprus?'

'Eleven months,' answered Nabil.

'Oh, then you must be residents here,' said the consul, without actually checking their papers. 'In that case, I shall try to help you. I shall send your applications to London and we shall wait for their decision. If you have any friends in the UK who can endorse your application, it might help.'

They left the Embassy in high spirits. Had the consul checked their passports, he would have noticed that they were in Cyprus on tourist visas for a limited time. God must have blinded his eyes! Grant promised to get the UK branch of his organization to write to the Home Office in London and fill out all the necessary paperwork for them.

The weeks went by. The Madanis waited for an answer. Renata's delivery time arrived and their second son was born by Caesarean section. They called him Mark, deeply thankful that both Renata and the baby were well. Two weeks after Mark's birth a pair of policemen turned up at their flat with a letter from the Immigration Office in Nicosia. Their time in Cyprus had expired; they were ordered to leave within 48 hours or face arrest and deportation.

This was a desperate situation. Had God brought them so far to abandon them now? What were they to do? This time even Richard and Grant had no help to offer. They tried the various embassies again, but everywhere the answer was the same: to process an entry visa for a Syrian would take at least six months.

In despair Richard suggested 'Let's try the Greek Embassy, Nabil.'

They hurried there, though it was Friday afternoon and the Embassy about to close for the weekend. Richard in his optimistic American manner demanded to see the consul, and was allowed in. He related the Madani saga and asked her to grant them tourist visas for Greece.

'As a Syrian, you must apply in writing and wait for it to be processed,' she said. Then, on second impulse, she asked if they had the necessary photos and money with them. She stamped their passports and gave them a thirty-day tourist visa to Greece. Handing Nabil the passports, she said 'Mr. Madani, I know nothing about you. This is the first time in my life that I have stamped a visa without first referring it to Athens for approval.'

'Thank you very much,' said Nabil, 'we will not disappoint you.'

It was a miracle! Nabil and Renata hurried home and packed all they could take with them on the ferry. Richard drove them to Limassol port and they boarded a ship that soon set sail for Greece.

It was the end of May 1989. The weather was extremely hot. The Mandanis were exhausted from the tension and all the running around. Their baby was not yet three weeks old, and Renata still felt sore, weak and tired after the birth. They had little money left after paying for the ferry tickets. But at least they had been given another chance.

Light at the
End of the Tunnel

The ferry-crossing was uneventful. Nabil and Renata sat on deck and watched the waves go by. They couldn't buy any food as they wanted to save the little money they had left for the unknown time ahead. Renata breast-fed the baby and secretly pumped some of her breast milk into a baby bottle. She added sugar and water and gave it to Piotr who drank it happily, not realizing its origin! Nabil tried to keep Piotr happy by playing with him and walking him around the ship to give Renata time with the baby. Neither Nabil nor Renata had anything to eat during the two-day crossing. Finally they arrived at Piraeus harbour.

Grant had asked an English believer, Linda, to meet them at the port. She had another appointment and could not be there, but had sent an American friend to collect them who did not know anything about their special situation. As he loaded their luggage into his van he asked, 'Which hotel shall I take you to?'

'To be honest with you, we cannot afford a hotel,' said Nabil, 'we really must find Linda as she is our only contact here.'

The American kindly offered to pay for their first night in the hotel, but Nabil refused. The American mentioned that there was a small spare storage room at the hostel where he worked which was vacant. They were free to use it until Linda was back in town. They gladly accepted the offer. The tiny, bare room had two iron bedsteads in it – nothing else. They stayed there for two days, waiting for Linda to turn up. With little to do, they walked around the neighbourhood, sat and talked, waited. The mosquito season was in full swing and there was little sleep at night. Finally Linda turned up and arranged for them to have a better room in the same hostel.

Linda had heard from Grant that, soon after they had boarded the ferry, he received a message from the British Embassy to say that their UK visas had arrived! Grant immediately rushed to the Embassy to collect them for transfer to Athens, but that couldn't be done. The visas had to be returned to London and only after being authorized could they be sent for collection to Greece. The consul wondered why the Madanis had left before receiving their visas.

'Were they deported from Cyprus?' he asked Grant suspiciously.

'No,' answered Grant truthfully, 'they left of their own accord.'

Grant contacted his organization in Britain and urged them to put pressure on the authorities to transfer the visas to Athens as soon as possible.

Those days were some of the hardest ones Nabil and Renata had to endure. They had almost nothing to eat. No one knew of their predicament. They watched enviously whilst the hostel staff fed their three voracious dogs with the most expensive imported canned dog food. A Canadian lady living in an adjacent room kindly gave Piotr some biscuits, but otherwise they survived solely on bread and water.

Every morning Nabil took a bus to the centre of Athens to the British Embassy, to wait there and hope that their long-awaited visas would finally arrive. On his first visit he was taken to a separate room for a tough security check when the staff realized that he was a Syrian. People were frightened of terrorist attacks and would take no risks. It was humiliating to be singled out for this treatment, the only one to pass through a special detection machine, be body-checked and peppered with endless questions. However, as he turned up day after day the staff soon came to know him well.

The thirty days in Greece passed. Still no sign of their visas. Would the authorities grant them an extension? What if they were deported and the visas arrived after they had left? Once again the Madanis went through an excruciating experience of utter helplessness. They felt like pawns in the hands of the powerful government bureaucrats. They had no control over their circumstances and, once again, could only cry to God for mercy and help. Even more than in Cyprus, now they felt that God had heard their prayers; they were comforted.

Linda helpfully accompanied them to the Greek immigration authority. She knew the people; they had often dealt with her own visas. Now she approached them and asked them to help the Madani family in their difficult situation. 'See Linda,' said the man in charge, 'I really respect you and the work you are doing in Greece, but the law says tourist visas can't be extended. They must leave the country and can then return and apply for a new one.'

Linda talked with him for a while, explaining that they were so poor that they could not afford any tickets. Finally he gave in. 'I can offer them no more than ten extra days,' he said, 'I do this only because I know that they are waiting for UK visas. I hope they get it during these ten days - but if not, don't come back to me for an extension, there is nothing more I can do.'

They thanked him and returned gratefully to their simple room. Once again Nabil fell into the routine of travelling to the British Embassy every morning, to be there when they opened at nine o'clock, waiting patiently until they shut for the day at one o'clock. 'Sorry, Mr. Madani, no news for you today, maybe tomorrow,' the staff would console him as they closed the doors.

The ten days ticked by. It was the last Friday. That morning, before leaving, Nabil had said to Renata, 'Renata dear, this is our last chance. If we don't get it today you must take the boys and fly back to Poland. I will certainly be deported to Syria - who knows what awaits me there. If I stay alive I will get in touch with you somehow.' They wept in each other's arms. Then he left for the bus station.

At the Embassy he again sat down and waited. Linda had promised to come and meet him there at noon, before the Embassy shut for the weekend. Around one o'clock the consul came out of his room and said, 'Mr. Madani, I'm sorry nothing has arrived so far. Have a nice weekend, maybe next week will be better.' The consul had no idea that this was their last day.

Nabil sat up as though he had turned into a stone pillar. He was in a state of shock. He explained his situation to the consul as he broke down and wept. The consul was embarrassed and said 'Just a moment, I can hear the telex machine in the other room. I'll go and check.' When he returned a moment later he held a piece of paper in his hand. 'Mr. Madani,' he said, 'how do you spell your name?'. Nabil spelled it out for him. 'Do you have all the necessary paperwork with you?' asked the consul.

Nabil nodded, but couldn't say a word. He had gone through so many extreme emotions that day, he fell over in a faint.

The consul helped him to a chair, fetched some water, and said in a fluster 'Don't worry, I'll do everything for you.' He opened Nabil's briefcase and rummaged through the papers, where he found the photos, the money for the fees and the other documents he needed.

'Now Mr. Madani,' he asked, 'who will meet you at the airport in London?'

Nabil couldn't utter a word, his mind was blank. Fortunately Linda turned up at that very moment and soon was in charge of the situation. She gave the consul all the information necessary, about the training programme the Madanis would be on in Britain and about the Christian organization running it. She got Nabil a cold Coca Cola to revive him and told him how happy she was that things had worked out for him at the very last possible moment.

'You can pick your visas up on Monday,' said the consul.

It was Linda who came to the rescue again and explained that the extension to their Greek visas was expiring this very day. It was the last possible chance to get their visas. Linda was British and could be very persuasive; the consul relented.

'Okay, I'll do it for you right now, even though it is Friday afternoon.' His holy weekend was violated, but he kindly filled out all the forms, stamped their passports and passed them to Nabil. 'I have given you the visas, but that is no final guarantee,' he said, 'remember there are still no diplomatic relations between London and Damascus. The immigration authorities at Heathrow could still cause you some trouble. Good luck, though!'

What a relief! Nabil felt he was walking on air. Another miracle had taken place. God had intervened again at the very last moment to sort things out for them! They really possessed valid one-year visas for Britain - it was almost more than he could take in after the many disappointments of the previous weeks.

When Nabil and Linda arrived back at the hostel, Renata looked up expectantly.

'Sorry Renata, no visas again,' said Nabil. He never understood what inspired him to play this cruel joke on her at that crucial moment. Renata broke down in tears, while Linda rushed up and reassured her, 'Oh no, Renata, he's just joking. You've got the visas.'

Then Renata was furious! She turned around and for the first time in their married life she smacked her husband hard across the face. It hurt. To an Arab it was doubly painful and humiliating if a woman should strike her husband and culturally totally unacceptable. But Nabil suffered it, penitent, for he knew he deserved it.

Now they had to move fast. They rushed into the city centre to buy their flight tickets to London. The earliest possible flight was on Monday but, as they had the visas for Britain, the Greek authorities kindly agreed to let them stay on for the weekend.

On Monday morning Linda drove them to the airport and they boarded the plane for London. Renata was so happy, she slept the whole flight while Piotr played and Mark cried. Nabil prayed almost the whole three hours from Athens to London. 'Oh God, let us get through immigration this time. Surely you didn't bring us this far to let us down.'

The plane landed at Heathrow airport and they

went into the terminal building to pick up their luggage. They headed for the passport checkpoints.

'Mr. Madani,' said the lady officer, 'I see you got your visa in Greece, why not in Damascus?' Nabil tried to appear calm and nonchalant as he explained that they had been touring around Cyprus and Greece for several months. She seemed satisfied.

'You are on a one-year Christian training programme, are you not?' she continued. Nabil nodded affirmingly. 'That's interesting,' she said, 'how come your name is Nabil Muhammad?'

Nabil quietly explained that he was a Christian.

'What are your plans when the year is over?' she queried.

'I'm sorry, but I really don't know,' answered Nabil truthfully.

'Excuse me, I have to refer this to the main officer in charge,' she said and disappeared.

Nabil felt his knees buckle. 'This is it Renata,' he said, 'we are finished.' But the lady reappeared in a short while, smiling. 'I have a problem,' she said, 'you are Syrian and your wife is Polish. It is unusual, I'm not sure I know which stamp to use.'

'Put on any stamp you like,' said Nabil with a sigh of relief.

'There you are,' she said as she handed them their passports. 'We'll contact you later. Welcome to Britain!'

God had answered their prayers. They had arrived in Britain. Nabil could hardly believe it as they moved to the exit where a member of the Christian organization was waiting with a van to take them into London. A small house had been set aside for them. They could breathe freely. No fear of deportation, no endless waiting for visa extensions - they had a whole year ahead of them!

Nabil started his work as an accountant one week after arrival in London. There was much he had to get used to – accounting in English, for one. He had always worked in Arabic before and needed to learn all the English terms of his profession. The people in charge, however, were very friendly and helped as much as they could.

Renata had a more difficult time adapting, as she had to stay at home with the boys while Nabil was away at work. She didn't know anyone in the neighbourhood and her English was still rather weak. She had practically no adult company until Nabil returned home in the evening. It was very frustrating for her and she craved going out to see the city, but by then Nabil was exhausted after a long day in the office. In some ways it was the most difficult year of their married life. They had to get used to 'normal' life and adapt to a new language and culture at the same time. Although the Christians at work and in the church they attended were friendly, there was no extended family to turn to. They had to cope on their own, sometimes with dire results.

Nabil and Renata both enrolled in English courses to improve their communication with their new British neighbours. The one thing they most enjoyed was the sense of security, so different from those tense months in Cyprus and Greece. The officials were more helpful and relaxed too - even at the Home Office. Things could be dealt with by letter and there was no need for urgent trips to government offices. They were treated with dignity – very different from the Middle

East, where bureaucrats imagined themselves to be gods who could treat ordinary citizens like dirt. Life in Britain felt like Paradise!

Of course, some things in Britain felt strange. After the gregariousness of the Middle East and Poland, British people seemed so uncommunicative, private and stiff. There was no sharing of personal problems, no spontaneous visiting of friends for a leisurely chat. It took them a while to realize people were actually quite friendly and concerned for them, even though they apparently did not express much emotion. In Syria, Nabil had been used to visitors stopping by any time of the day for a chat or his family going out to visit other family and friends - no one was ever alone, there were always others to talk and share the gossip. In London they learned to live quietly inside their own home, day after day, with no one stopping by for a visit. They were lonely. It was difficult to get used to this way of life.

Later that year the Christian organization relocated to a smaller town in the northwest of England. The Madanis moved again. Slowly they settled down, found a church where they were gladly accepted and helped. For the first time in their married life they had a secure place to stay, a stable job situation, a friendly church where they could get to know people. They savoured the taste of stability.

Another source of joy was that Renata's mother could come and visit them freely and enjoy her grandchildren in England. The collapse of the Communist regimes of Eastern Europe now made such travelling a straightforward matter. Of course there was the matter of renewing their visa once a year. Every time they wondered whether they would be allowed to stay in Britain for another year. . . .

At the end of their first year the Home Office granted them an extension for another year. That was good news. The second year went by. This time their vicar suggested they apply for political asylum in Britain. He knew the local MP and arranged for an interview with him. The MP was impressed by their situation and promised to help as best he could. He wrote on their behalf to the Home Office, who contacted them with a wad of forms to fill out. They did so, and in April 1991 they sent in their official application for asylum.

The Struggle for Asylum

Having filed their application for political asylum in the United Kingdom, Nabil and Renata settled down for a long wait. In December 1992 Nabil was asked by the Home Office to attend an immigration interview at Manchester Airport on the 10th March 1993. He was also asked whether he needed an interpreter. Nabil confirmed the invitation by recorded mail, but declined to accept an interpreter as he felt confident speaking and understanding English. He asked that the director of his Christian organization would be allowed to accompany him. A month before the interview was due the Home Office contacted Nabil again, asking why he hadn't confirmed his acceptance of their invitation. Thankfully he had sent his reply by recorded mail and Nabil was able to assure them that he had indeed responded to their letter. They later admitted that his reply had been misplaced.

Nabil and Renata prayed and received much advice in the weeks that the interview approached. They were tense weeks of great apprehension. What would the outcome be, they wondered. It seemed as if so much depended on this one interview!

Finally the day arrived and Nabil drove to Manchester Airport together with his director. During the drive they reviewed the situation and discussed how they would present it to the interviewing officer. They wondered whether the officer would be sympathetic to their case. On arrival they found that the Madanis' vicar had also kindly driven all the way to the airport to offer his support and help. However, the

Home Office refused to allow him to see Nabil; sadly he had to leave without being able to exchange any words with them.

A young Asian lady approached them and introduced herself as a Home Office official, asking Nabil to identify himself and his companion. She asked them to wait. After about fifteen minutes she had found an interview room. The small office contained a table and four chairs. The lady officer then told them that she had appointed an interpreter for the interview. Nabil and his director objected, saying they had declined the offer of an interpreter. She insisted on the presence of an interpreter and, after some hectic consultation, they agreed to let him attend so as to avoid any possible misunderstandings.

When the interpreter arrived Nabil was shocked to discover that he was a Syrian citizen, a Muslim who had residence in Britain. The lady conducting the interview was a Pakistani Muslim – things looked gloomy indeed and stacked against him! Had this been arranged on purpose? The officer insisted that Nabil's director was only supposed to listen in as an observer and was not allowed to comment or participate in the interview in any way. Nabil was very worried; he hoped this was not going to turn into a nightmare.

The interview started at 9.30 am and continued till 6.30 pm with only a five-minute break. The officer started the interview by asking personal questions about Nabil's identity, occupation and work. Then she went on to ask about the reasons for the Madanis' application for political asylum. Nabil felt bombarded by the many questions and weary from the emotional strain. His mouth was dry from nervousness but, though the lady and the interpreter had some tea, nothing was offered to Nabil or his companion. Her questions seemed to go into great detail on unimportant and irrelevant questions, such as how much Nabil had earned in 1982 (ten years earlier) and how he had spent it. It was ridiculous to be expected to remember such things. It really felt as though she was trying to put psychological pressure on him. Most frustrating was her effort to present his employment as incompatible with his request for asylum. Nabil wasn't really well informed about this aspect of employment of refugees by charitable trusts. His director, an expert on that, was not allowed to speak. Finally, after much negotiation, she allowed his director to explain the situation.

Then she questioned Nabil about why he had become a Christian and how it had changed his life. Nabil sensed that she felt humiliated as a Muslim when he explained how he had found the Christian faith superior to Islam, especially as it was in front of a fellow Muslim, the Syrian interpreter. Another suspicious detail they noticed was that the interpreter was writing down the whole interview. When questioned about that, the interviewer merely said that he was an independent interpreter and that they had nothing to fear from him.

The interview was a harrowing experience. Nabil and his director both felt it had been consciously set up in such a way as to humiliate them. Nabil was sure that once their interviewer had submitted the report of this interview to her superiors, there would be no chance of the Madanis receiving asylum. A week later they visited their solicitor in Birmingham to complain about the way the interview was conducted. The solicitor was shocked at what she heard and advised an immediate complaint to the Home Office in Birmingham. She agreed that it had been set up in a deliberately antagonistic and insensitive way, apparently arranged to prejudge the matter and elicit a negative decision.

After much correspondence between the solicitor and the Home Office, they were finally informed that the Madani application was under consideration. There was nothing more to do now but to wait patiently and trust in God.

One year later the Christian organization that Nabil was working for was awarded a prestigious 'Successful Business' prize for the North of Britain. The director of the Christian organization that Nabil worked for attended the ceremony, and it just so happened that the Home Office Minister was the celebrity invited to do the presentation of the prizes. After the ceremony the director was invited to a dinner and found himself seated next to the Minister. Seizing the opportunity, he proceeded to tell the Minister about Nabil's case and his anger at the biased way in which the interview had been conducted. The Minister asked the director to send him a personal report that fully explained the situation.

A thorough internal investigation at the Home Office followed the arrival of the director's report. In May 1995 the Minister personally wrote to the Madanis to inform them that he had decided to grant them political asylum in the UK until May 1999, when they would be able to apply for permanent residence status. This was indeed good news! The Madanis were overwhelmed with such relief, gratitude and joy. God had granted their request in answer to their prayers and a journey of waiting which had taken seven years! Now they finally could put down roots.

During the following years the Madani boys started school. They soon were fluent in English and very happily settled. They joined the choir of the local cathedral and went on to take part in a choir tour to perform in Germany and Poland. The family now had many good friends, including some from the Middle East who seemed like members of their own family. The Madani family could also travel abroad and their first trip was to Poland, to visit Renata's mother and the rest of her family. It was a time of great joy and a happy family reunion.

By 1998 Nabil had spent eight years working in the accounting department of the Christian organization. He had gained valuable experience in the British way of business transactions and relations, while at the same time contributing to the organization's success and growth. However, it seemed that God was calling him to something else, to a work where his particular strengths and knowledge of Arabic languages and culture could be used. A Christian organization with a very particular ministry to the people of the Middle East contacted him. Nabil and Renata felt God's clear guidance when Nabil was offered a position as assistant to the Director of Finance. He would also be involved in the media department where his Arabic skills were sorely needed. What an exciting new challenge!

Of course it was not easy for the Madanis to move again, but they wanted to serve God where their abilities could be best used. And, this time they moved within a framework of secure asylum status, waiting only for the time when they may apply for permanent residence.

Finally, do the Mandanis ever look back with bitterness at the 'wasted' years and hardship? Never.

Rather, they look back in amazement at the way God had faithfully led them and provided for them throughout the turbulent years since Nabil first came to believe in Jesus Christ. At times the pressures seemed almost unbearable, but God always provided a way out. Instead of trusting in high officials and good contacts, they have come to trust in the best friend anyone can have, the One who can plead with God the Father himself on behalf of mere persons. The Madanis have come to believe in the power of prayer. Through faith in Christ they have found a loving Father who never stops caring for his children. From the unknown God of Islam and the remote God of Catholicism they have come to know Christ as their personal Saviour and Lord. They have walked from the shadows into the light, from the dark tunnels of legalistic rituals into the bright inner place of communing with God, from working hard to earn merit with an apparently capricious God into the security of being 'in Christ' – sheltered and covered by his blood and righteousness, filled with his Spirit. Above all, they know that in Christ their sins are forgiven and they are assured of a place in heaven.

Nabil and Renata love the words of Paul, who expressed what they often feel: 'Forgetting what is behind and straining towards what is ahead I press on towards the goal to win the prize for which God has called me heavenwards in Christ Jesus' (Phil,3;13,14).

Nabil still loves his own country and people. He believes that, as Jesus was born and grew up in the Middle East, it should be easier for people from the Middle East than for westerners to understand the parables and stories of Jesus and the hidden meanings behind them. The Madanis' greatest desire is to be reconciled with their family in Syria. They pray for it regularly and wait expectantly.

If you have been challenged by the real-life story of Nabil and Renata and want to know more about the Christian faith or want to pray for the growth of the Christian church in the Middle East –

Please get in touch with Arab World Ministries:

* AWM, PO Box 51, Loughborough, Leicestershire, LE11 0ZQ, United Kingdom
e-mail awmuk@awm.org

* AWM, PO Box 96, Upper Darby, Pa 19082, United States of America
e-mail awmusa@awm.org

* AWM, PO Box 3398, Ontario, N3H 4T3, Canada
e-mail info@awmcanada.org

* AWZ, Postbus 57, 1619 ZH, Andijk, The Netherlands
e-mail awz@a2bmail.net

* MENA, BP317, 26003 Valence Cedex, France
e-mail bureau@mena-france.org

* Alternatively, leave your name and address in the guest book at www.awm.org